CW00447538

Andrew Gilbrook

is

An Ordinary Guy
An Unknown Spy

How to start, be smart, and end your career in MI6

Photography Andrew Gilbrook

Cover design: Codruț Sebastian FĂGĂRAȘ
fagaras.office@gmail.com

1. The End

I squint against the morning sunlight as I stagger out into the fresh air after days in the dark interrogation room, my hands bound behind me, my legs struggling to support me. One of the three black men guarding me shoves me in the back to keep me moving. He shouts something in Chokwe, the local language in the province of Moxico, the eastern extremity of Angola. Another shove forces me to the right. After days of brutal beatings, I am covered with bruises, but their blows no longer hurt. I'm in a bad way.

I had identified the head interrogator as a Russian foreign operation's and intelligence professional, probably SVR or GRU, but he hadn't cracked me. I had stuck to my story as being a member of the United Nations Angola Verification Mission (UNAVEM) team, which, while technically true, served only as a cover to my real mission. Somehow, though, he knew my real identity as an officer of the UK's Intelligence Service, MI6. But how did I know? I'm not going to find out – in a few minutes I will be dead.

I'm being marched into the woods nearby, far enough in so that the smell of my rotting body won't offend the occupants of this camp. I am to be shot and left for the animals to squabble over for breakfast. These human animals won't bother digging a grave; this country is too uncivilised for that. They are laughing, still drunk and high after a night of drinking Cuca beer and chewing khat. I keep walking toward my death.

Four hundred yards from the camp, we reach a small clearing. A hand grabs my filthy bloodstained shirt collar and yanks me to a halt. One of the men shoves me around to face them and pushes me backwards, against a tree. I stand, looking at them enjoying their cigarettes, I hope they can shoot straight and make my end quick. I settle back against the tree as my thirty-three years on this earth flash before my eyes.

I don't want to die here. My daughter is only a year old. I want to see her grow up. I want to see my wife Julie again. I lean into the tree, my bound wrists press against the rough bark. Almost immediately, a stinging ant bites the base of my thumb. Fuck it! Is there anything in this country that doesn't cause pain and discomfort? Even though I'm about to die, I shake my hands to rid myself of this biting nuisance.

Cigarettes finished, the three begin to prepare their weapons, pulling back the bolts of their AK47s.

This is it. I'm going to die in just a few seconds, no rescue, no help.

Go on. Do it! Do it NOW!

2. Early Days

My childhood was quite normal I think. I was born in London 23rd October 1955. My first real memories are of the day my parents and brother Steven, two years older than myself, moved home in 1959. We got lost on the way to Maple Cross near Rickmansworth, Hertfordshire. I couldn't believe my dad didn't remember where our new house was. Once we did find our street and house our furniture and belongings didn't arrive until the next day. A neighbour was kind enough to lend us some blankets and we all slept on the floor in our new home, a three-bedroom semi-detached house, with a nice large 100 feet long garden. Maple Cross was built to accommodate an overflow population from London, most people either commuted or found new jobs when they moved there. Now it is just inside the M25 circular road around London.

I loved living in the countryside, I spent most of my days playing in the fields and woods, and in those days there was little traffic so the kids of the village could quite safely play in the streets. With my friends we would build tree houses, come autumn we'd make castles in the fields from the straw bales, light fires and make camps in the woods nearby. One friend and I used to spend hours, if not days teaching ourselves how to follow animal tracks, working out how to move silently through the trees so as not to scare the birds and animals away. All good stuff that would pay dividends later, once I became an intelligence officer, where being the invisible man was often an essential skill.

My parents didn't ever have a lot of money to spare. My father at that time worked for the Royal Insurance Group in Acton, and my mother was a housewife, but soon my dad would start his own business when the Royal Insurance moved to Liverpool, my Dad didn't want us to live in a big city.

By the time I left school, I'd never been to a restaurant or knew how to write a cheque and pay bills. Most times I was shipped off to my grandparents when Mum and Dad went away on holidays, so I never travelled. All my friends seemed to have the latest toys, I rarely did. In the summer my friends would go on day trips to the coast in a big neighbourhood group, we never joined them. On those occasions I'd just take myself off to the woods alone, moving quietly, to get close to the multitude of birds and animals one could never normally get near. I remember one time I managed to get within 30 feet of a large stag deer before it saw me. It stood staring at me for a bit before walking away without alarm or panic. I'd learn how to snare birds, prepare and cook them on a small fire rather than walk all the way home for lunch. I spent many hours teaching myself how to shoot air-rifles, fixing and zeroing the telephoto sight. I think I became quite expert, I could hit an ice lolly stick at 60 feet with a .22 rifle.

Many weekends and school holidays were spent finding and cutting off pram wheels and making what we called trolleys, charging down our street with bows and arrows that we had made ourselves, firing at each other playing Cowboys and Indians. I wouldn't say we were feral kids, but we did do a little vandalism, for no real reason other than we could, and always get away with it. In those days many sheds and garages had roofs of asbestos corrugated sheeting. We discovered if you threw pieces onto a bonfire in a short while it would explode. I'm sure that would be a practice well and truly frowned upon these days.

I learnt the difference between rich and poor, as just a few miles away was the stockbroker belt of Chorleywood and private estates such as Loudwater and Heronsgate. The big houses and posh new cars in those areas let me know there was always people much better off than our family and that those types rarely mixed with the likes of us living in the council estates at Maple Cross. My street though, the houses were mostly owned and mortgaged properties with a few at the bottom of the street privately rented.

I did complete my childhood without breaking any bones falling out of trees or drowning in the gravel pits that stretch for miles from Rickmansworth to Denham. In those days before they all became private fishing lakes, we could witness Pike taking ducklings, grass snakes, and catch sticklebacks or nine eyes in the streams that fed the watercress beds in West Hyde.

3. School Days

I started my education at West Hyde School but then soon moved when it closed, into the newly built Maple Cross JMI at the end of my street. I didn't like it much, I hated being stuck indoors. I did occasionally become spelling king or won gold stars in the weekly maths tests. My best times though were when I was in Miss Willox's class. She was a large formidable woman, and very strict. When she sat at her desk at the front of the class, she always sat legs open and one could see her knee-length bloomers - not a pretty sight. I realise now, that despite her slaps and "chivvies" as she called them, she was a very good teacher. She was a keen ornithologist too. There were a few of us that could visit her home in Heronsgate at weekends even, to watch and learn all the birds in her garden. Around Maple Cross, we could see some quite rare birds, Tree-creepers, Bee-Eaters, even a Ring Ouzel to name just a few.

The Headmaster Mr Naylor or "Naggy" Naylor, as we called him, was also a good man and teacher. He wrote plays for school productions. I can still remember the words and story-lines of a few even now. One year I invented a new Christmas decoration made by bending two coloured paper straws into triangles, tying them together with cotton so that they formed a six-pointed star, He was so impressed he got the entire school to make one each and hang them on the school Christmas tree. I think I was always more practically minded than academic, although I didn't really struggle with maths or English. We weren't taught languages at junior school, something I found to be a disadvantage later in secondary school. In sport, I was the only boy that could stand on his head. Parent's days were often entertained by my gymnastic demonstration. One year I stood on my head with my legs apart, while other kids dived between my open legs, landing with a somersault on the mat behind. Something my mother later said caused her to break into a sweat watching. At the time I didn't understand why, I think I do now.

One year we had an exchange teacher from New Zealand, Mr Gundy. He knew nothing about maths, we spent the entire year learning everything New Zealand. He was a great guy and made a lasting impression on me, I think I can still sing "Pokarekare Ana" or "Now is the Hour" in Maori some fifty-five years later.

Because of my birth date, I and a few others had to stay in the top class for two years, as the cut-off date for moving up to secondary school was September. This meant we became more like school prefects and having to learn things twice meant we did well in exams to grade us for next school. In the end, I was offered the option of taking the eleven plus exam, I passed and I was told my next school would be Rickmansworth Grammar School. I didn't want to go there at all. I knew I wouldn't do well there, plus all my best friends were going to William Penn Secondary School, Mill End. I wanted to be with my friends. A few other kids were also going to "Ricky" Grammar, but I hardly knew them.

September 1967 I started my life as a "Grammar Grub". My parents couldn't afford the school uniform. In a second-hand shop, mum found a green blazer for me. It was a lighter green to the correct uniform, so I stood out as different right from the start. I certainly felt different.

By now I had a reputation for being a bit of a fighter, word had got around to the other kids, so no one ever tried to bully me for being different. Realistically, I didn't fight anyone just for the sake of it. I hated bullies, still do, and would never take any nonsense from them. In fact, my reputation grew while at Junior School, anyone being bullied seemed to come to me, point out the bully and I would sort them out street style. Once the bully knew I was looking out for the poor kid being harassed by them they tended to leave them alone. I certainly knew I couldn't win every fight, but I would make sure the bully would feel some pain before I'd get whooped myself. I just never showed fear and they knew I'd get stuck into them. I had a big fight one day with the toughest kid in school. I couldn't beat him, but he couldn't get me to surrender either. Despite getting hurt myself, I had hurt him enough to admit to others I was a tough cookie. From then on they gave me respect and my word alone was enough to stop any other kids getting bullied if they asked for my help.

I remember one rainy day our P.E. lesson had to be in the gym. Our teacher Mr Barret, a short man as wide as he was tall and muscles everywhere, decided we would have a wrestling competition. Two boys would enter a circle of mats, the first to get pushed or thrown out of the circle lost the match. Each boy was partnered with another about the same size and weight - except me. I was partnered with the tallest and fittest boy in our year, Ralph Carpenter. Apparently, my fighting reputation had reached even the staff at this school. Mr Barret was obviously expecting big things of me. On the whistle, I ran straight at Ralph, who grabbed me by my rugby shirt collar, spun me around a couple of times, let go and I flew out of the ring. Mr Barret looked less disappointed when I stood up laughing after my flight and crash landing. I think my reputation dropped a couple of points but I survived.

I enjoyed P.E., but I seemed to have stopped growing, which put me at a disadvantage in rugby. We weren't permitted to play football as Mr Barret thought the game was for wimps, which may be true. So I alternated between rugby and hockey playing in either team at away games just to make up numbers it seemed to me. Even though I played in most home and away games, I was never awarded a cap. The cap system was never explained to me and to this day I don't know what I had to do to be awarded one. Lads that I had played alongside in the same team all filed up to the stage in assembly to be applauded and awarded a cap, yet I was always left out. I don't understand why, what didn't I do?

We never won any inter-school sports, simply because for some reason we always played the year above us, so in the second year, we played another school's third year. None of us could understand why, and we became quite despondent about it. So instead of trying to win, as a team, we would pick out someone from the opposing team that we didn't like the look of, and, each of us did our best to have a go at ripping the shirt off the lads back. Some of our victims ended the game with almost no shirt left. It was the only way we could get any pleasure from our losses with scores such as 84-12, quite humiliating.

Sports days in the summer, I was quite good at athletics, I seemed to be good at sprints and long-distance running. One year I even won the triple jump by one centimetre from the favourite boy. I was also pretty good at javelin but gave it up after a practice session, when I did my usual run-up, as I concentrated on hitting the mark for the throw, I lost control of the javelin which had turned ninety degrees and as I put all effort into the launch throw, it hit me with a huge whack on the back of my head, pretty much knocking me unconscious, I executed a perfect face-plant into the ground and the spear landed point down, still in my hand about half an inch from my ear. I never threw another one ever again.

As for cricket, forget it.

In my second year at "Ricky" School, we were placed in Maths forms according to our grade after the end of year exams. I was in the bottom grade, yet because the teacher was so good and I liked her, I did quite well. Unlike other maths teachers, she took time to help individuals that struggled with certain aspects of the subject. My favourite subject was Physics because it is mostly practical logical stuff. In chemistry, I just couldn't grasp chemical formulae at all, I didn't get it and no one bothered to help. Biology was ok, the teacher was hateful, but she was quite young and always wore very short skirts. In languages, it was compulsory to learn French. I didn't like French, mainly because I never saw the point and the teacher was quite hateful. He could clearly see I was not trying, so his tactic seemed to be to do anything to humiliate me and make me feel useless. He didn't have to try hard. I was, however, keen to learn German. I had an uncle, an ex-para that I liked, he lived in Germany, and while stationed there he had met and married a German girl. Quite something in those days, so many people still had strong memories of the war, his parents, my grandparents were firmly against it. Anyhow, I liked Uncle Peter and his wife at the time Ziggy. I always thought one day I would like to visit them in Bünde, so I wanted to make some effort to learn the language. I asked the school language department head if I could give up French and learn German instead. The answer I got was, "As I was rubbish at French I would be rubbish at German too and they didn't want to waste time with me". Always encouraging my teachers! So I bought some books of my own and taught myself. I did get to visit Peter and Ziggy in Germany. I travelled over with Peter by car and came back all the way from Bielefeld by bus alone, at 14 years old and never having travelled abroad before. I was put on the bus with no food or water for a 24-hour journey, to be met in London starving hungry and dehydrated by Mum and Dad, who showed little concern for my plight. But the German language I picked up in those two weeks have stuck with me, and I was quite capable of helping my two daughters when they were at school with their German homework.

The third-year at secondary school is always the year kids get naughty and a little cocky, the year most pupils either get caned or expelled. I think only one pupil in my year was expelled, after being caned. I recall that he was caught smoking, with quite possibly not 100% tobacco in his cigarette, he was that type. A nice guy, a bit rough around the edges, but popular, and I remember several girls crying after hearing the news. This year was also the year I started to play up too. I realised I stood no chance of ever getting good grades in any exams. My parents had the attitude that university was a waste of time and that everyone should get to work to earn money. So I felt I had nothing to aim for.

Because of the distance I lived from school, I had to catch a bus at about 6 am, as the next one would arrive with about ten minutes to spare before the start of classes. If the bus was late, so would I be, and the detention for that was never appreciated, as I felt it wasn't my fault. Jo Franek and I came up with a plan. A classmate and very good friend, who lived in Chorleywood in a huge house had the same problem. He had to catch a train first to Rickmansworth with all the commuters on the Metropolitan line, then catch a bus to the school. So we decided to arrive early to avoid these problems. This meant we got to school about 7 am a little uncomfortable on cold wet days. So, before we left school the day before, we would leave a window in our ground floor classroom slightly ajar. We could then climb in and sit in the warm doing our homework. We never did anything wrong or bad, we just wanted shelter and spent the time productively. Jo was way better than me at school work. So he did his work and I would copy. After a while, the prefects patrolling inside the school would catch us in our classroom, which was a big no-no before 9 am. We would get caught and thrown out into the cold and rain. So we took to hiding in the classroom cupboard. This was quite large, there was even a desk and chair in there so that during the day sixth formers could sit and do extra studies. Our classroom was in the French department, so I assume these sixth formers were studying French. Eventually, the school caught on that we were leaving the window ajar, and the janitor would come after we left at the end of the day and close the window. We thought we could outwit him by leaving a window open on the first floor, in the geography department. We'd climb a drainpipe to a flat roof above some cloakrooms, then another drainpipe up to the window. Here we'd have to do a leap of faith from the drainpipe and grab the window frame. Once we had a good grip let go with one hand, with the other open the window fully and climb in. From here after closing the window, creep downstairs and into our classroom and into the cupboard. Because the downstairs window was being locked, the janitor had no idea of our new route in. Until, one day, Jo, after doing the leap of faith, hauled himself too enthusiastically up into the not quite so open window, and cracked his head on the window frame, causing him to fall. He had a severe cut on his head, with no one around yet, there wasn't anyone I could call for help. In those days mobile phones hadn't been invented yet so Jo lay on the cold floor a long time bleeding before help did arrive. Later that day, I was interrogated by my form teacher as to what we were doing. He didn't seem to understand we were just cold, wet, did no damage or harm and simply got on with some work each morning. We didn't get into trouble for it though. It was deemed Jo had suffered enough, but it had to stop.

April Fool's Day that year was hilarious. All five classes in my year got up to such funny tricks, all harmless and well planned. I think the teachers got it, and some even managed to laugh along. I remember the class next to mine, the boys removed all the screws from the door hinges, so they fell in when the teacher opened them. In my class, most of the kids were more of the nerdy type and weren't quite so bothered. But I didn't let the class down. I asked one of my classmates a few days earlier to help. He was particularly good at chemistry. On the day, he produced, as requested, an amount of 2,4 dinitrophenylhydrazine or 2,4-DNPH a yellowy red chemical. This is a chemical often used in school A-level practicals, some schools stocked it. It's used to identify organic carbon-based compounds called aldehydes and ketones. Dry 2,4-DNPH is friction and shock sensitive. For this reason, it's supplied damp or 'wetted' when a school purchases it from a chemical supplier. It's important that it's kept wet, so the storage advice is to keep it in a sealed container, which is itself kept in an outer container filled with a small amount of liquid. If the chemical is allowed to dry out, there is a risk of a small fire or explosion. Johnathon brought it to school in a jar inside a jar. The jar inside suspended by elastic bands so that it wouldn't bump and the inner jar was filled with a fluid to keep the chemical wet. I thought it was a very clever homemade design. Johnathon gave me the jars and wanted nothing more to do with the caper. Just before our English lesson and before the others entered, I got into the classroom opened the jars and spread the chemical around the classroom, some on the window sills and quite a bit around the teacher's desk and floor. Mr Daykin our English teacher began the class. As the grains dried, the window sill first as it was in the sunlight, started to explode. In small amounts, it sounded like cap guns going off with a crack. I could see Mr Daykin becoming more and more annoyed and agitated by the noises. Eventually, he shouted "All right, who's got the cap gun". Everyone looked around at each other as only I knew what it was. Crack! Another went off. Everyone was puzzled. "Alright

Gilbrook," he said to me, "Outside". I had to go stand outside the classroom. Of course, the cracks didn't stop so he couldn't be sure it was me. I felt a little indignant that he chose me as the culprit, correctly of course, but with no evidence. The little explosions were going off all day, in fact, a few still the next day. I never owned up to it, but I learnt a huge lesson. Never stand out from the crowd. While everyone in the room was looking mystified as to what was going on, I was the only person laughing, that's why I was singled out, even with no proof of guilt.

Standing outside the classroom was a dangerous place to be. The Headmaster, Mr Morrill, would often patrol the corridors. Anyone found stood outside, must have been naughty, resulting in some kind of punishment. I saw him coming further down the corridor. By the time he reached me, he found me staring into my locker opposite the classroom looking most forlorn. Asking what I was doing outside the classroom, I proclaimed the contents of my locker had been stolen and my books and equipment had gone. I had simply emptied it into another, as in those days the lockers were wooden with no locks. It was a major crime, to steal from a locker. Anyhow, seeing how I was so upset (great acting on my part), he took me back into the classroom and instructed Mr Daykin to find me some new books and everything I needed to resume class. My teacher was red-faced fuming at being reprimanded. From that day forward it was a hate-hate relationship. He never really bothered to teach me anything more and would only speak to me if he thought it was a question or something I didn't know, in an attempt to humiliate me. I didn't care, the other kids in the class took sympathy on me, always showing concern that this teacher would always pick on me, for some reason, I happily took the sympathy.

Outside school, at the age of fifteen, Jo, from school, and I taught ourselves to drive. Jo did a lot of car maintenance for his family, one of his sisters had bought a Fiat 500. After working together doing whatever repairs we had to do, of course, the car would need to be road tested. Jo would normally drive, but one time, on a road that crossed Chorleywood Common he offered to let me have a go. It wasn't so difficult, except that model of car didn't have synchromesh gears. To anyone that doesn't know, in a normal car these days, when using gears, cars have a gearbox that can move up and down gears without any crunching. Simply stated, a synchronous transmission matches engine speeds to the rpm's of the gearbox so that as the clutch moves the throw-out bearing the two engaging gears will mate smoothly without grinding. In the Fiat 500, the gears have to match for speed before you can slip into the lower gear, a method called double de-clutching. It took a little practice but I got it quite quickly. Neither of us had a license or insurance.

After school, a few days per week, I would go work for a few hours with my father at his new business, a printing company. This gave me enough money to buy a motorbike. A Honda 50. With no clutch, it was easy to drive. The school wouldn't allow me to ride to school, so I rode from home and left it at the back of a shop just opposite school, where the owner, Michael Thame a friend of my father, permitted me to park.

As I approached the age where I could leave school, I decided I would quit at the earliest opportunity. My mock 'O' level exams had gone badly, and it was clear to me I could never pass anything and I was wasting time at a Grammar School. It seemed to me that if you were a high flyer and destined for university, you got all the help you needed. For someone like me, not stupid, but practically minded, there was only humiliation and the total lack of any care by the faculty. There were a few teachers I did like, but to continue was pointless in my mind. My mock 'O' results were a joke. In French, my friend Jo managed to pass his paper to me to copy. I copied the lot. He got a result of 84%, I got 2%. Apparently, I'd written each answer one line down, so got all the right answers in the wrong place. 2% was for getting my name correct I think. I told Mum and Dad I wanted to leave school. They, for some reason, were against it. I didn't understand this as it was clear they were against further education and wanted me to work to bring money into the house. I was flummoxed by this attitude. I think it was the shame of me failing while all the other kids around were aiming high. They refused to write a letter for me to the school to say I was leaving. It was left to me to do it myself. I decided to speak to the teachers personally. I went to my form teacher Mr Drew first. I told him I was going to leave the day I was legally permitted at 16. He told me that this was the best thing I'd done since I got here. Next, I went to my Physics teacher who I did like. He tried to persuade me to stay, but I explained it was pointless coming for just one lesson, it wouldn't get me anywhere. He was sad to see me go. My Maths teacher, a lady I liked a lot, did have the patience to get some of the harder subjects into my head. I did appreciate her efforts. She cried when I told her I was leaving. All the rest could hardly speak to me and gave me no encouragement to stay. Finally, I went to the Headmaster to tell him I'd spoken to all the teachers that needed to be told, and it seemed fairly unanimous that it was better I left, to allow the others that wanted to learn to get on with it, without mini-explosions going on around them. He asked me what I was going to do. I told him that I had little idea what I was capable of doing, but that I was probably going to help my dad, who was just starting up a printing business. It wasn't planned, but I had to say something. He asked me if I had ever thought of working for my country. I had no idea what he was on about, so replied that, as I was going to have to pay taxes I would probably be working for them all my life. I added that if he had any idea himself what he thought would suit me I'd appreciate the advice. He said he thought he had a good career in mind for me and that he would check a few things and would write to me shortly.

As it turned out, a letter arrived at home for me quite soon after, inviting me to an interview in London. Not saying much more than that, as the letter seemed quite official it did intrigue me.

So I went.

4. Interview

On November 23rd 1971, I travelled from Rickmansworth Station to Lambeth North Station, London, a journey of about an hour with one change at Baker Street Station to the Bakerloo Line. My destination was Century House, 100 Westminster Bridge Road, the then home of the Secret Intelligence Service (SIS), commonly known as MI6.

The letter I received, following the school resignation chat with my Headmaster, gave me brief instructions on how I should keep my business with SIS secret, but that I may tell my closest family or spouse what I was doing. I chose not to tell anyone, as I felt sure there was no way, I would pass the interview, thus save some face and not disappoint my parents again. The dress code was "grey man" smart. I didn't know what this meant, I had no grey clothes at all, nothing other than jeans, as I never went anywhere 'posh'. I decided the best option was school trousers, school shirt, grey tie, and shoes, with a kind of black cotton/denim jacket for warmth against the November cold. In those days November was cold, there was often a frost lasting most of the day, we don't get cold weather like that these days in England.

I found the entrance quite easily, but as I had allowed far too much time to travel to London as I hate being late, I decided to wander around outside for a while until a more suitable time for my appointment to enter the building. About 400 yards away, opposite the station, down Kensington Road, is the Imperial War Museum. I walked there in just a few minutes, I didn't go in, outside the front gate was an ice cream van, I bought an ice cream cone to stop the beginnings of hunger pangs. I ate while looking at the two big guns in the garden facing out from the entrance of the building before returning to Century House.

Fig. 1. Century House, London. Then headquarters of MI6

A modern looking 22 story building, I entered not knowing what to expect. Immediately approached by two security guys, set up on two ordinary tables either side of the doorway, it seemed to be a temporary arrangement, surprisingly. It was the first time I'd ever been frisked, bringing home to me that perhaps this place might be something special. After checking I was on the visitor's list they directed me to a waiting area, I sat for just a few moments before a lady arrived. She stayed behind the revolving bomb-proof doors, completely made of clear Perspex glass or something stronger, she called my name and waved me through the revolving door to where she stood. I thought I should start taking mental notes of my surroundings, quite rightly, I had a feeling somehow it would come up later.

The interview was surprisingly easy. After completing yet another form, more sections requiring my personal details again, which I'm sure they knew anyway, there was a very simple informal chat in a small room with another woman, presumably from HR. I talked about my interests, which at that time were few, and what I knew about the service, which was nothing. It was stressed several times that it was imperative that I always answered questions honestly, they preferred the truth, even if it was something that might normally be considered bad, such as, had I ever taken drugs, which I haven't, ever. It was thought that passing through the university system it was unlikely that one could get through without experiencing drugs at some point, it wasn't frowned upon at all, and wouldn't necessarily result in a fail today if I admitted I had tried them. I moved on to another room where there was what looked like an exam room at school. Desks in a row with papers prepared and laid on each desk, I thought, maybe others were expected, but none arrived. I was invited to sit at a desk and complete what seemed a psychological profile test of some kind. There were about 100 simple scenario questions, which, toward the end, I started to lose concentration and interest in. The problem for me was, it seemed to be all scenarios I had never faced, such as, how did I cope with someone collapsing in the street, what did I do in that situation? I hadn't experienced anything like that yet. So I made up answers how I thought I might act because I didn't want to appear stupid, probably that was a mistake. Toward the end, I started to think maybe I should be honest, and simply answer "I have not experienced this", I completed the paper with most answers completed this way. The time given to finish the test was quite tight, so I rushed through the questions. I think this would have usually resulted in a fail, but maybe because they had already decided they wanted me, I passed anyhow. I don't know how these psychological things work.

Back to a third person for another easy informal chat. The guy here wanted to test my powers of observation. He asked me to describe the man that brought me from reception to this department. I started by saying, first of all, it wasn't a man but a woman, which he seemed surprised at. I described her from top to bottom easily as I had made mental notes expecting something like this. He said he then knew who I was describing but couldn't understand why she had fetched me and not the guy that was assigned. Not my problem. He asked if I had any questions myself. I had a million. I asked if I could have a look round to see what went on here. I wasn't permitted. I asked what role they thought they had in mind for me. He claimed he didn't know, I'm pretty sure he did. But he did describe what facilities were available for staff, such as canteen, gym and gun range. I asked about pay. He did give me examples according to role, rank, length of service and so on. It seemed pretty poor compared to how well paid I thought it should be. None the more for that, it was better than anything I could expect anywhere else. It was suggested that I should continue to work in my current job until I heard more. The whole thing had taken about two hours. I was then informed that if my application was to continue there would be background checks, including immediate family and any significant others, and only then would I hear if I was going to be a successful applicant. I was a little surprised because I had thought it was them that wanted me. But then I suppose I could fail if they found something they didn't like about my family. I had to be a British National, I didn't know anyone in my family that wasn't. I left quite exhausted. I travelled home thinking I had no choice but to go to work with my dad in his business.

My Dad's business was very small, renting a garage at the back of a parade of shops in Mill End, Hertfordshire. My father said he needed me to help, I'm sure my wages put a strain on his finances. I started working for him immediately. He taught me the basics of letterpress, typesetting, and finishing. I operated a Heidelberg Platen Press and a small electric guillotine. Everything was hands-on and incredibly boring. I was paid £6.50 per week, a wage well below the normal basic rate. When I complained about the poor wages, it was explained to me that one day the company would be mine and working for next to nothing was an investment in my future, let alone help the company grow with less of a financial strain upon it. I wasn't entirely sure printing was my future as it was so boring, but I did almost enjoy the practical aspect of it, especially later, as the company grew, and we began to print using the lithography method, and more chemicals and processing was involved.

It took six weeks for the checks and processing to be completed at MI6, a letter dropped on my parent's doormat addressed to me. I had been successful! I was invited, should I wish to proceed, to a second interview. I continued to hold back from telling anyone, as it seemed to me there was still a possibility I could fail.

After what seemed a lifetime waiting with excitement, I was on the train again, travelling back to Century House. This time I was interviewed more intensely by, as it turned out, my mentor to be, John. Dressed quite casually John was easy to get on with and I liked him, later in life, we continued to stay in touch and often, with our wives, had dinners together. After a break for coffee, a whole mass of paperwork had to be completed, some seemed so irrelevant, and, why did I need to fill my name and date of birth and National Insurance number so many times? The formalities took ages. The mess hall was well equipped and a very busy place, but it seemed to me, was mostly secretaries and admin staff here, with no sign of any spies.

After a good lunch, which John paid for us both, he asked if I'd like to have a look around the building. I couldn't help feeling excited now, surely this meant I have been accepted. There were rooms equipped with computers of all kinds. Computers, were as yet not a household item, seeing these quite advanced systems was of huge interest to me. I had no idea of their capabilities. In those days rows of Winchester drives with the large 24-inch- and 14-inch-diameter media were typically mounted in standalone boxes resembling washing machines. Newer, smaller diameter media drives using 8-inch media and 5.25-inch media were also evident, I later found out that at that time data was being transferred from the large disks to these smaller, faster and higher capacity machines. I could tell I was going to love working with such advanced computers systems, for a person like me there would be little chance to be able to work with such technology anywhere else. Of course, I had very little idea what these machines were being used to store.

Upper floors, were corridors of offices, decorated in business-like colour schemes, not dull, but efficient magnolia or white walls and oak wood door frames. Secretaries busy at typewriters, some looking up to give an acknowledging smile, others were concentrating and taking notes on their telephones. It was obvious to me that this was a place where serious work was done. John led me down the corridors, often stopping to chat with people, introducing me as a prospective officer, everyone seemed quite happy and friendly. Working our way up the floors, missing some floors out to avoid repetition as several were much the same, we finally arrived at the top floor, where the offices were more hushed and better appointed, I was taken into one office and introduced to 'C'.

I learnt the term 'C' originates from the initial used by Captain Sir Mansfield Smith-Cumming, RN, when he would sign a letter "C" in green ink. Since then all chiefs have been known as 'C'.

Sir John Ogilvy Rennie, KCMG, was the 6th Director of the SIS (MI6) from 1968 to 1973. When appointed, his brief was to reform the organisation. I learnt later that it was his association with my Headmaster Mr Morrill, and, because of my practical abilities, skills at cheating, lying, apparent nerve, yet obviously not as dumb as I made out, placed me as a good candidate for his purpose.

Post World War 2, there were mumblings that MI6 recruited only those in the old boy networks, Oxford and

Cambridge Universities in particular. MI6 was presented as an ever-present and incestuous web of prep schools, old-school-tie bureaucracies, and smoke-filled Soho clubs. It was said Kim Philby, Britain's most notorious Cold War traitor, was able to pass secrets to Moscow because British Intelligence was 'staffed by ill-disciplined and inept upper-class twits' - twits who were prepared to turn a blind eye to the misdemeanours of one of their own. The Cambridge 5 Spy Ring is a very good example of how those traitors passed information to the Soviet Union during World War 2 and were active at least into the early 1950s. Yet none were ever prosecuted for spying. The term "Cambridge" refers to the recruitment of the group during their education at Cambridge University in the 1930s. This particular topic is covered extensively in other good well-researched books and is not a subject I want to cover here, but could be considered the reason as to why I believe I had been selected, from a most unusual background. I believe initially I was more an experiment and my expected failure could be used to prove the mumblers wrong.

It became a major worry, to the USA especially, that British Secret Services could no longer be trusted. Something had to be done within the Security Services to, in my words "lower the tone" of the establishment. My innocence in such things at the time probably helped me survive. I had no idea how these places worked or operated, I had never read a book on any Intelligence Service, in fact, I don't recall reading any books at all. The Beano was my limit. Perhaps my naiveté was a particular attribute that was being sought, after all, from the moment I would be recruited everything I learnt, would be what they wanted me to learn. My entire knowledge of SIS was James Bond movies. A total misconception, far from pistols, unarmed combat or irresistible sexual magnetism, a normal SIS officer's primary tools for motivating foreigners to do what he wants are bribery, bullshit and in certain circumstances blackmail. The only Bond-like quality a normal SIS officer will be required to show is the ability to drink heavily and remain functional, as any diplomat must on the embassy cocktail circuit. I guess my ability to think quickly, especially when I need to save my skin, to have no qualms about telling the odd lie, were skills perfect for the role. The downside to my appointment into the service was that I had absolutely none of the people networking that all the "upper class" types had.

In order to prove the old system of recruiting for MI6 should be favoured and maintained, I formed an opinion shortly after beginning work for SIS, that I was being set up to fail.

To some extent, I have to agree with the old system despite my position. In the SIS world, there can be nothing more valuable than networking, to always know someone in the right place, or even to know someone that knows someone. The public school and Oxbridge Universities must be the best places to form your network base, after inherited networks. To this day, I have no idea what was expected to be the outcome of my employment in SIS. To my mind, and I found this out very quickly, I was merely an experiment, a joke that many of the "toffs" quite openly sneered or laughed at. Once I realised this, it simply served to make me want to prove them all wrong, my background with dealing with bullies would pay off.

I wasn't defending just myself, but in my opinion, all of my social class. I believe and can find no evidence to the contrary that I was, and still remain, the only recruit never to pass through any university or private school system. Whether that means I failed later in my career. As my story unfolds, it remains to be seen.

After my second interview, I returned home to continue work at Peter Gilbrook Printers, to await further instructions. It was now that I broached the subject to my father. I told him that I had been offered a good job. It was always a good idea to have some employment somewhere as a cover should the need arise, so I explained the nature of the job and that I needed to continue working with him, but also needed a lot of time out. Never one to express emotion to me my father hardly reacted at all. I wasn't sure he believed me. I told him I would continue to work with him until I received further instructions, and then, we could decide from there how we could work the two jobs together. I told him that my employment at SIS would need to remain a secret and that I would leave it up to him whether he told mum. My mother was a difficult problem, she could never be relied upon to keep such a secret, and it was of some concern to me how to deal with her knowing. I asked Dad how he thought it best to approach her. He decided there and then to not tell her, if we couldn't keep my employment with MI6 from her it would be all over Maple Cross, and Hertfordshire by tea time. That is how my MI6 career remained all his life, he never revealed what I did to a single soul. He assured me that he could manage some kind of cover for me. It absolutely worked so well and for so long.

After a week or two, I received instructions to report again to Century House, where I signed in, with John, now appointed my mentor, signed all the papers necessary, including the Official Secrets Act, I was given papers to study which set out the offences related to spying, sabotage and related crimes. I wanted John to know that he would be working with a blank canvas as far as I was concerned, I knew nothing of what was expected of me. He kindly reassured me that I had been selected for precisely those reasons and that having studied my reports he was confident I would do well, so long as I paid attention and realised this was a serious business. His character was such that I always felt at ease in his company, and, often despite his serious warning, we had many a good laugh together.

We went together to visit "C" in his office. I was surprised and impressed how much Sir John knew about me, I didn't have to explain anything to him, and he seemed to know everything, even what I had eaten for breakfast that day. I told him that I was feeling like a fish out of water here, I had no idea where to start or how. He informed me that I would be attending "Spy School" to learn the trade and after I completed the courses, he had something in mind for me to do.

I left more nervous than before. I was most probably so scared by the time I disembarked the train at Rickmansworth Station, I felt I had already a few grey hairs on my head. Being frightened is no bad thing, it makes one sharper, less likely to make errors, and as long as one can control any fear, learn to use it in a positive way.

Instructions arrived shortly after telling me when and where to report for training.

5. Spy School

I'm not giving any secrets away in this book, and it is public knowledge, to anyone interested in these matters, 296-302 Borough High Street, London was a 'spy school' for SIS Officers. The Ministry of Defence has now moved out, but the building still remains. Until the 1990s, the establishment stood opposite Southwark police station in a MOD building, a quite unremarkable building, one could easily walk past it not caring what went on inside. Called a 'non-field training headquarters' rather than a spy school, it would teach spies the techniques that they would use in their work. Another establishment building was Fort Monkton, the secret service training base on the seafront just outside Gosport, Hampshire. Here, new recruits to Britain's Secret Intelligence Service are taught their art-form of the more physical kind, including my favourite, pistol shooting, by a retired sergeant-major. I won several contests, while my air gun exploits as a young boy were useful, most public schoolboys had already experienced and fired real guns, but I think my natural ability came to the fore.

The chances are, however, is that spies will never get to use this skill because the world of spying is almost nothing like its popular portrayal. Real-life James Bonds, for instance, don't get to run around like mavericks these days, running riot around cities in car chases, or getting into gunfights. Nor do many intelligence officers get to have sex with their sources of intelligence. "It isn't normal to sleep with a target. If you have to, it means you are not in control," said one former British operative. Someone once summed up the role of the building: "Essentially,

James Bond would have been trained to kill in Fort Monckton, Hampshire and then would have been taught what documents to complete, when he had killed someone, at Borough". I did attend some other specialist schools, these places will remain secret.

The London school, while interesting was not so much fun for me as the practical lessons that I enjoyed so much in Gosport. It wasn't easy by any means, especially for me, compared to the other "students" who had been recruited from normal university routes. Initially, I did find myself sitting alone as someone not worthy of the company of those from private school backgrounds. Some individuals were working class, in fact, there was quite a good cross-section of society in the classes, but I was the only person so young at seventeen and so uneducated. I was age disadvantaged by a good three years, if not more.

Many of the lessons were of the initiative type. It has been written about in several other books notably Peter Wright's "Spycatcher", I believe his book was the first to reveal Fort Monkton as to what its purpose really was. He wrote about one of the skill tests given at Gosport in which the student had to obtain an unknown person's name, address, and passport number. He accomplished this using great initiative when a couple of girls in a bar were asked if they would like to accompany him to France on his yacht. As Gosport is close to many marinas filled with yachts it wasn't that usual for skippers to be looking for crew. The girls were told their passport details were required for customs in France. Easy! In my class, people were given various tasks. The one given to me sounded simple, but then once I thought about it I realised how difficult it could be. I was told that by the following week, I had to plant something blue on one of my classmates, it would be my choice to which person would be my victim. Easy I thought. But then it dawned on me, that as everyone knew each other's task, they would all be looking out for me, not wanting to be the 'victim', and for me to fail the test.

The following week, on the day we all had to produce the fruits of our labours for the test, everyone was carefully avoiding me. It was obvious I could only plant something blue onto one of my classmates on the actual day. No-one wanted to sit next to me or pass closely to me. On that day I became the subject of a number of jokes sitting alone, working alone, to be avoided at all costs, I couldn't get near anyone. At the morning coffee break we trouped off to the canteen, which was a simple room, self-service, one made their own coffee and helped themselves to biscuits, or make some toast etc. Not one person would come near me. I said "ok guys I get it that no-one wants to come near me. You all sit over there, I'll make the teas and coffees". They were giggling like children that I would not be able to plant something on any of them while they were watching me like a hawk. I stood alone in the kitchen area preparing teas, coffees and biscuits for them all, looking quite forlorn. After the break we wandered back to the classroom, my so-called colleagues hanging back letting me walk in front of them, so I would not make a last-minute attempt to plant any kind of blue item on any of them. I love being the butt of jokes! In class everyone produced the results of their particular task, some were quite ingenious. Explaining how they achieved the aim of each task. My turn came. "OK, Andy, can you reveal who, if anyone, you have planted a blue item onto, and how did you complete the task, please," my lecturer asked. Everyone in the room was checking pockets, shoes, even hair in some cases. Happy that I was going to fail my task, there was a lot of giggling among them all. "Actually," I said "I have planted something blue on Peter", Peter looked horrified I had beaten him, "and Mark", pointing at Mark, equally mortified. "Oh, and Mike, in fact, everyone here in this room, including you," I said pointing at my lecturer. They all looked mystified, how had I done it? What was it? None of them could find anything in their pockets. The lecturer asked me "What have you planted?"

"Well," I replied, "During tea-break, I put a few grains of Methylene Blue Powder onto your biscuits, in your teas and coffees. In a few hours, you will all be pissing bright blue". Methylene Blue has several medical uses. It is a safe drug when used in small doses. Before using it on my fellow students, a few days earlier I tested it on myself, I took about 30 grains of the powder in water. The dose was a little strong. On the day I guessed about ten grains would suffice. I also found there was a slight narcotic effect that made me a little hyperactive and I spent the afternoon after taking the powder telling non-stop jokes. The effect at toilet time was amazing and hysterically funny. My pee was bright sky blue. It is also a great April fool's joke as my wife can testify, I recommend it. Some of the guys got the joke, others thought I was taking a risk with their health. I didn't care, after the treatment they gave me that day, they deserved everything they got. Next day, classmates were reporting good results, some said they found it hilarious having such bright blue pee, a few didn't get the joke at all. My lecturer reported I had received full marks. No previous students had ever been quite so imaginative with that particular task, or for that matter, had ever managed to plant something blue onto (or into) every student including himself. After that day I felt a little more accepted among my peers, a couple even congratulated me.

Had I been the lecturer on that day, I would have given me a fail. The point of both the tests mentioned in this chapter was that the student should learn the ability to persuade. In the passport test, the only solution was to trick someone into believing that by giving the information required, something good will happen, i.e. a nice sail to France. The proper solution to my test, I believe, would be to plant something blue on a comrade by persuading someone to come onto my side, and help me to pass. In my case, I had no real friend in class. They kept themselves away. I should have selected a person that I could have persuaded to come onto my side, knowingly take a blue item from me and place it upon their person for me. My solution, while hilarious, could have led, in a real situation, to the chemical being detected, identified, and potentially cause an international incident, place the UK as a nation prepared to injure, or worse. Of course, I know that now after years of experience, but my solution does demonstrate to some extent the danger of out-casting a person, a company or nation. Backed into a corner they will bite. I think today we have seen examples of that and the international reaction to real events such as the attack on Sergei Skripal, and his daughter Yulia, in Salisbury, which left them hospitalised for weeks. Georgi Markov, September

1978. The Bulgarian dissident who was poisoned by a specially adapted umbrella on Waterloo Bridge. As he waited for a bus, Markov felt a sharp prick in his leg. The opposition activist, who was an irritant to the authoritarian communist government of Bulgaria, died three days later. A deadly 1.7mm-wide pellet containing the poison ricin was found in his skin. Alexander Litvinenko, November 2006. The fatal poisoning of the former officer with the Russian spy agency FSB sparked a major international incident. Litvinenko fell ill in November 2006 after drinking a cup of tea laced with radioactive polonium. The United Kingdom does not want to be seen to be involved in such dirty business in public.

As generous as my lecturer was, maybe because I did actually achieve the aim of the test in an original and complete way, he felt I should earn a pass. Maybe he saw I had little chance of persuasion in the situation I was in with the other students, and that the solution to the problem was a subtle underhand blunt stick approach. Maybe I had to pass because I was destined to be the fall guy in the establishment, who knows. At the end of the day, in my opinion, I hadn't achieved the point of the lesson, I should have failed that test.

A skill we had to learn to a high level was the ability to track and follow a subject, both on foot and in vehicles. Having spent so many of my childhood days tracking and stalking animals I found it quite easy to adapt my methods. My character is such that I can quite often enter a party or something similar, walk through a room full of people and be completely unnoticed. I don't know what it is about me that makes me invisible to people, it can be a useful skill, as well as upsetting when people can't remember me. We were taught how to work in teams and alone. We had to learn to be the subject being followed too. Being the subject, there are methods to detect and avoid being followed. We were taught when playing the target, to walk, for instance, down a high street and to have a theme. You walk looking into shop windows that sell a certain type of product, so you become a man looking for a shirt or shoes. I never thought these tactics were of much use when one is a known target, in that case, evasive tactics might serve one better. I was always of the opinion that one shouldn't become a target in the first place, it means you've lost your anonymity already and can easily be picked up again later if you evade your followers. Once we became proficient at this skill, there was, unknown to us, one final test where we would follow a target alone. The target would duck down an alleyway in an attempt to lose the identified stalker. What the stalker doesn't know is, this is a trap. There would be some guys in the alley waiting for the stalker. They would grab him, bundle him into a vehicle and give him a good roughing up, in a quite realistic manner, I have to say. The kidnapping is then followed by imprisonment and interrogation - all very realistic and quite uncomfortable. The guys kidnapping the stalker would be Special Forces and have no qualms about throwing very realistic punches. It's all intended for the student to experience real capture, including sleep deprivation and being placed in very uncomfortable stress positions. It was, of course, to evaluate how the student copes with such treatment. None of the trainees had any idea that the tracking of the subject was about to lead to a few days capture, interrogation and pain. Quite a few failed at this point in the course.

Unknown to us, this experience would happen near the end of the course during the day. One by one, about an hour apart. Each of us was told to go wait by the Portsmouth to Gosport Ferry terminal in Gosport. We had been given a description of the subject to follow who was going to arrive by ferry from Portsmouth. We were to identify him, follow him and produce a full report on where he went in town and who he met, if anyone, without being spotted. None of us suspected at all what was about to happen. I arrived at the ferry terminal, maybe I should have gone to the ticket office to look at the timetable. I thought it a bit obvious, anyone trying to spot me would pick me up easily. Instead, I sat on a low wall at the back of the new bus station next door among some trees, I could easily see the ferry depart on the other side of the estuary. I hadn't been given a time of arrival for the ferry that the subject would be on. At that time of day, the ferry ran every 15 minutes. I saw the ferry pull away from the landing on the other side, it took about 4 minutes to cross the water to the Gosport side. People disembarked, although a little distance from the ramp, I could make out each person, I didn't want to risk moving closer, in case anyone was looking out for me. I couldn't see anyone fitting the description. No panic, I carried on waiting, trying to look like one of the many locals and tourists around the place. I didn't want to move my location, so I waited for the next ferry. About 15 minutes later the next ferry arrived, passengers disembarked, still no subject. The ramp cleared of people, and the next line of waiting passengers started to walk down the ramp onto the ferry to cross to Portsmouth. There, as the passengers started to board a lone figure fitting the description walked up the ramp. He continued to walk straight, momentary moving behind the bus station out of sight from where I was sitting. I started to walk around the far side of the bus station from where he was, bringing him back into view as he neared the roundabout at the end of the High Street. I walked along the bus platform between the buses and the waiting rooms where there was plenty of cover, looking around for any other characters that were trying to pick me up and follow me too. At that time in 1973 Gosport High Street was still open to traffic, it has since been pedestrianised in 1991 but there were the beginnings of the works to convert it providing good cover for me to use. The whole area was being renovated after so much war damage, many of the ruined buildings were under reconstruction still. He entered the High Street which runs west from the ferry, four shops up, he paused, and entered the Woolworth's store. I moved north from the bus station, around the north side of the roundabout, so that I would end up on the opposite side of the High Street from Woolworth's. On the roundabout was the Ark Royal pub, I entered a door to move out of sight, from here at the top end of the bar I could clearly see Woolworth's doors. I ordered a drink while I stood watching the shop opposite and took my jacket off, a quite natural action in the bar, but realistically it was to change my look, now I was wearing a jumper. I hung my jacket on a hook under the bar so that the barmaid would not see I had left it behind. I would come back later to collect my lost property. This also gave me a chance to see if anyone looked as though they may be following me. No sign of anything odd so far. If the subject decided to try to duck out the back of the shop, it was better to give up, as it may mean I had already been compromised. But a minute or two later and only a few sips into my drink he reappeared in the doorway. Pausing slightly to take a look round, he turned left and continued west up the High Street. As he was about to disappear from my view from the pub, I placed my drink on the bar and left by the door into the High Street to follow. He stayed on the same side of the road, pausing occasionally to look into shop windows. I was sure he had not seen me leave the pub. Making sure never to pause or waver whenever he stopped, I continued walking at the same slow pace using window reflections to watch him rather than look directly at him. He also entered a bank halfway up the road, but it was easy for me to fake a stop at a shop and again use the reflection to watch out for him to reappear. Taking about 15 minutes to walk almost to the far end of the street. We were at a junction with Clarence Road. I believed I had still not been identified following him. On the southwest corner of High Street and Walpole Road is a social club (now Gosport Conservative Club), along the west edge of the club, there is a narrow alleyway leading to staff car parks and then on to South Street behind. Here he quite slowly and deliberately turned left and walked down this alley. I was sure he did this to make sure that I followed, even though I was still convinced he hadn't seen me. I didn't like the look of this at all. Something wasn't right. He could have walked down the road just before the social club building. I wasn't going to follow him it would expose me for sure. I could easily have walked toward South Street from where I was, but that would have meant a sudden change in direction and slightly doubling back on myself. I chose to continue on to the end of the High Street at a much faster pace and hope to pick him up again in Creek Road or South Street. It was a risky strategy, but I did indeed spot him much further away on South Street walking east. This meant he had effectively doubled back on himself. It didn't make any sense and I felt very uneasy that maybe he had spotted me. He turned left into Thorngate Way, a road that doglegged north then east behind the police station (now closed). Again, I was some distance away and I felt sure he had not seen me. I crossed the road and walked briskly east down South Street, ducked behind the flats opposite South Cross Street because by now he should be appearing from Thorngate Way into this street. Edging around the buildings using the few trees as cover, there was no sign of him, he was still in Thorngate Way. I walked further down South Street about an extra 200 yards and dodged left into Coats Road, another road that doglegs north then west. This put me in a road that heads toward where he should be and I should be able to see him somewhere at the rear of the police station. Using the car park the east end of Coats Road I could peer around the corner to try to spot him. Indeed, there he was, at the rear gate of the police station that led into the car park for police cars. He was talking to four other rough-looking men. They seemed confused and looking around for me but in the wrong direction. They hadn't expected me to get on the east side of them. One guy was flapping his arms as if to say "where is he". I had no idea that the trap was meant for me to be captured and bundled into their van parked in the police station car park out of public view in this quiet road. I waited a few minutes to see what they did next. In the end, they all got into the van and drove away. I had successfully followed the target from the ferry to a point where it was impossible to follow any further. I had no backup to call so I couldn't follow in a car. A strange exercise I thought, far too easy. I had no clue that in fact they had failed to kidnap me for the interrogation phase. I returned to Fort Monckton unaware I wasn't supposed to be free. I found my instructor who wasn't amused. I thought I would be debriefed, giving a full account of the afternoon's work. Instead, I got a roasting, I don't know why as I had evaded the target, I evaded the other men that were meant to grab me as I walked past the gate of the police station and bundled me into their van. It was explained to me what was meant to happen. So what should I do now? Go give myself up? I was told to wait, while he went to find the interrogation team. No, the surprise had gone, I now knew what the afternoon should have led to. I was given a partial pass for evading everyone involved. Did I think it an unfair result, surely I had been successful? As a result of my success, I never did endure what everyone else had to. I spent the next few days, reflecting on my luck, while my fellow trainee spies were being subjected to abuse. When the other guys returned from days of imprisonment they looked a right mess. They had been stripped of all clothes, put into stress positions, deprived of sleep, quite realistically beaten until they cracked and gave the information their torturers wanted - while I sat in comfort enjoying hot meals, tea and biscuits and spending time in my favourite place, the shooting range. If anything could serve to restore the class divide that did. My response to my critics "fuck off and learn to tail someone properly".

I attended various other courses around the country before I was given a pass with credit, not the best in class, but I was happy with that, despite missing out on a beating. I returned home to begin my work as a fully qualified spy.

6. Starting at MI6

1974 saw me arrive at Century House SIS Headquarters in London with the rank of Officer. I am not entirely sure what they liked about me, but I have always had a good memory for small details. I can forget people's names two minutes after being introduced to them, but I retain a lot of seemingly unimportant information which can be important when dealing with a mass of paperwork on your desk or when you are out in the field trying to remember what your brief was. I arrived at the security check-in where I was on the visitor list but this time directed to an office to the right from the security tables. In this room sat a lady who, on checking my ID, gave me my staff pass, and instructed me to always wear or carry it while in the building. John was called on the internal phone network, and five minutes later met me in the lobby waiting area. With a big smile, he welcomed and congratulated me and led me upstairs. He took me to my own office, a simple room, on the fourth floor. There was a desk with a computer terminal linked to the SIS network, a few cabinets, a small safe and a couch with a low coffee table. There was a through-door to an office where I was introduced to Karen my secretary. With that John announced he would leave us to get acquainted and that was it.

I was not yet nineteen, had my own office and secretary, and, no idea what-so-ever what I was supposed to do next. Karen was without a doubt the most professional person I have ever met. Unfortunately for me, she was also stunningly beautiful to distraction. Blond shoulder-length hair tied back in a ponytail. Immaculate makeup. Dressed in a white shirt, dark navy jacket and matching knee-length pencil skirt. While I couldn't believe my luck that I would be awarded such a vision, I knew her looks would be a distraction. Her sense of humour matched mine perfectly. I don't know if the secretarial pool matched staff so that they would work together well or not, if this was a dating game, it would have been a perfect match. Except she was about 7 years my senior. I must have stared too long, with a smile she said "I should close my mouth now" after John left the room. She held out a perfectly soft hand to shake. Shy as I am with girls, our handshake was a little on the brief side. She had the kindest eyes and smile. After the brief introductions, I shrugged and said: "I have no idea where to start, what do I do? I've been given no brief". Karen replied, "Not to worry today, I will take you around the building and introduce you to the people you should know. I'll show you how to use the computer network to the best advantage, ignore everything you've been taught on that, there are better ways. I will make an appointment for you to meet "C" sometime today, hopefully, he will give you a brief. Do as he asks, do it professionally and you will be ok here. Would you like coffee or tea?"

"Tea, white with two sugars please" I stumbled my reply, now shaking with nerves. It had dawned on me I was way out of my depth and I told her so. "It's your first day, no one would expect you to be an ace, take time to settle. Let's go to the canteen and meet a few people". With that she placed her notepad and pen onto her desk, we walked through to my office, locked the interconnecting door, I wondered why. Were there thieves or spies about!

We took the elevator down to level one where the canteen was. I looked at her, she smiled back. I informed her that I had been to the canteen before and that there seemed to be so few Officers, she told me that the building was mostly admin staff. It seemed reasonable, why would Officers expose themselves to the risk of being identified entering Century House. It made sense to me.

At the canteen we collected tea and coffee, I was too nervous to eat. We sat at a table where two of her colleagues were sat. "May I introduce Andy, his first day" she added in a whisper. "Andy this is Elaine and Penny, they have offices on our floor too", I shook hands with them both, nice young girls but nowhere near as attractive as Karen, unsure what to say, better I say nothing and just smiled. Penny broke the ice, "Andy, what do you think of Karen, isn't she attractive?" Elaine added, "Yes, all the men here fancy her" they both giggled. Karen stopped the line of conversation, "Not very professional ladies. Come on Andy let's get back to work". Well, that was a short break. Back in our office, Karen proceeded to show me the computer network system and how to get the best from it. I had never seen such an information source. Computers in those days were still in their infancy. This system was something else. Of course, I had had lessons on how to use it in Spy School, but it didn't show me half of what was being demonstrated to me now. There was so much to learn here. It was nice to sit close to Karen and she didn't move away if any part of our bodies touched. We spent some time going through protocols and procedures by lunchtime my head was overloaded with information. As I was about to suggest some lunch, her phone buzzed, it was "C's" secretary confirming an appointment at 14:30 that afternoon. I asked if I could eat at my desk and asked her if she could fetch what she thought was good to eat, before leaving she made me a cup of tea in her room and brought it to my desk. While she was away, I set my safe code, then stood to stare out the window for a few minutes in quiet reflection. What was expected of me? Am I really capable of doing this job in a manner equal to others that have gone before and those that are here now? I watched the outside world go about their business until Karen returned with lunch.

After my food, Karen's phone buzzed, John Rennie "C" was ready to see me. I took the elevator up to his top-floor office, where I was shown into his office straight away. He held out his hand to welcome me to my new job and motioned for me to sit on one of the two sofas, arranged so that they faced each other with a low coffee table between. I declined another tea. He talked a while, telling me what was expected, that his door was always open should I need advice. I should get at least six aliases and continue to perfect my languages. I asked if I had a brief so that I could begin work proper, a little unsure that I was ready to get into real work right away. My only concern was that I had never travelled overseas, my one trip to Germany as a fourteen-year-old was my entire experience. He told me that he would arrange a trip for me. He could see that I was still shy and nervous and told me that I should take time to get acclimatised to my new surroundings and that he did have something in mind for me, but not just yet. We sat a short while talking, he seemed unhurried and willing to give me all the time I needed. I'm sure he was using this time to asses me, to figure out how I thought and worked. We ended the meeting by agreeing to meet again, at a time when he thought I would be ready for my first brief.

I headed back down to my office, spoke to Karen, I told her I was heading home and not to expect to see me for a few days. I had no idea how she occupied her day, but she always seemed busy. I had rented a small top floor flat in Linden Lea, Leavesden near Watford, quite close to what at that time was Leavesden airport owned by Rolls Royce, now Warner Bros. studios. A friend's mother worked for a rental agency and had found me this nice little bedsit flat, one room, a separate kitchen, and quite a large bathroom, it also included a garage. If anyone had done their maths properly they would see I couldn't afford to live there on just my wages from my printing job, where, I was now earning £7.50 a week! The flat cost £45 per week plus bills. I also purchased my second car after my first car an Austin Mini finally died. My pride and joy was now a white Triumph Dolomite. To rent the flat I was merely asked if I thought I could afford it, no checks, nothing!

Next day I went to work at Peter Gilbrook Printers, again. By now it had grown and Dad had acquired the garage next to his and knocked a door through. He had a huge contract to print two hundred and fifty thousand sponges for Johnnie Walker Whiskey Company. The job would last months, and he had taken on a part-time worker to help too. The sponges were dehydrated and like a rough thick piece of card. We'd print a red Johnnie Walker logo on them on a semi-automatic letterpress machine. The sponges had to be fed into the machine by hand as they were irregular in shape. A laborious job, it gave me a chance to think about how I should begin my secret career and demonstrate I was capable, while I was working at the printing company. I began to form a plan while I stood shoving sponges on and off the press.

7. Xerox

I had a friend that worked at Xerox photocopy machines in Uxbridge, a large office block a few miles from where I lived and worked. I had heard somewhere that photocopy machines had a hard drive or ROM chip that kept an image of each copy that was made, but that this image was not deleted by the machine after the item being copied was printed. Copiers scan your documents to create replicas and then they store that information on an internal hard drive. That means a drive you can't easily access and may not know about, could be holding some of the most sensitive company data that you've got. Estimates say that a multi-function copier can hold as many as 25,000 documents in its memory, maybe more. I didn't know if this was true. I made a date with Janice, a girl I had liked back in Maple Cross Junior School, but were separated when I went to Grammar and she went to Comprehensive School. She agreed to meet me, after a catch-up, I broached the question about the copiers. At first reluctant, she did, after a short time, give me the information I needed, and yes it was true. I explained that if the information got out it could have dire consequences for her company, which she could understand. I asked her if it would be possible to get hold of a copy of the design sheets of a machine, so that I could develop a way to delete the drives, thus saving her company a red face if it were ever found out they had this huge flaw. This device could be used to provide the company engineers with a method to delete the hard drives at each service, thus Xerox will not need to admit to all their customers the fault in design, and I would get rich by manufacturing the hard drive deleting devices. Of course, this is only what I told her in order to get blueprints of the machines. Surprisingly she agreed, as she had easy access to everything I required, so long as I never admitted where I got the information from. A week later I had copies of the designs of every machine they made! A brilliant piece of espionage by Janice, if ever there was one. It can be said she was my first agent recruit. With this, I approached another friend Steve from Grammar School days, who worked for a computer design company in Watford, he saw the potential of what I was doing. He agreed to design and build a simple device that could plug into the machine's drive. Apparently, many of the models used the same drive. He built one device for me with a few different plugs connected to a battery-powered mobile drive that could first copy all the data, and then delete the drive in the Xerox machine. I now had the capability to copy hundreds of thousands of images of photocopied papers (and a few office party backsides!). We tested the device at Steve's place of work in a photocopy machine. We downloaded about fifteen thousand images. These could now be transferred to a computer by simply plugging the device into the back of almost any computer at that time.

I wanted to test my device for real. One of the companies Gilbrook Printers did printing work for, was Rolls Royce in Leavesden, where they manufactured small engines for helicopters. Next time I delivered some printed stationery to Rolls Royce it was easy to get through security at the gate. I delivered the packages of printed stationery, left the stores and entered a random office where through the glass windows in the corridor, I could see there was a copy machine. I announced to the guy in the room I was there to service the photocopy machine. He pointed to the machine against the wall, without hardly lifting his head from the drawing board where he was working. I opened the machine, plugged in my device and downloaded over ten thousand images. Closed the machine, stood up after a few minutes pretending to service the machine and announced all was well and good for another six months. Spying was going to be this easy.

In those days modems were incredibly slow, I couldn't send the information to Karen at Century House London, so the results of my theft had to remain with me for a few days. Next time I visited Century House I plugged it into my computer and uploaded the images. I told Karen what I had done, but I wanted to keep it secret from my colleagues in MI6. Karen and I agreed we should create a database and work out a method of filing to aid retrieval in an organised manner. Karen was happy to work out a system for me on an independent, firewalled computer system, to keep it all to ourselves.

Although I didn't go to Century House very often, I did maintain communication with Karen by phone for more or less daily updates, we always knew what the other was doing. We gradually built a relationship that was more than just professional. She knew I didn't have a girlfriend, I was very shy when it came to girls. I knew she didn't have a boyfriend, it seemed to me that she wasn't really looking for one, concentrating on her career more than her personal life, my secretary was always available, day or night 24/7.

I needed to expand my enterprise. I contacted Janice at Xerox again. I told her I had come up with a method to delete the stored images during servicing. I made up a story to get her to supply me with all the documents needed to make me look like a Xerox Service Engineer. She was completely on board with me, not realising I could see all the documents after uploading. A few days later I could pose as a legitimate copy machine engineer with ID and all the papers necessary to appear I was contract servicing the machines.

The next few weeks saw me a couple of days a week visiting companies in south-east England and downloading the contents of their photocopying machine drives. I visited Marconi North London, British Aerospace, London and Farnborough, Lockheed Martin, London, Martin-Baker near Uxbridge, Private Banks in London, High Street Banks and Building Societies, Investment Companies in London, Share dealing companies, and many, many more. I couldn't count how many images I had stolen. Probably several million! Poor Karen had trouble indexing so much data, but she was happy to be kept busy and always greeted me with a smile. Eventually some years later, as technology advanced, I would send the images by Internet from home, rather than visit Century House, but for now, I would take my drive device to my office for Karen to upload.

I had an appointment with "C" a few months after I started work, on one of my rare visits to SIS London, he asked me what I had learnt and had I found a way to be productive. I said "Yes I had very much found a way to keep myself busy", he asked me what I had been doing. Not wanting to reveal my crime, I gave him the answer "Doing my job, spying". He questioned whether he would see results of whatever it was I was busy doing. "Of course", I replied, "when the information I am gathering is as complete as I can get it, he would be given a full briefing". Lying through my teeth, I wasn't going to tell anyone, even him. Walking back to my office to retrieve my device after Karen had finished the latest upload, passing an open office door, I overheard a conversation between two men I didn't know, and they were talking about one of the companies I had raided. I popped my head through the door, I said I could help with the information they required. Looking down their noses as I had come to expect, one of them asked what I knew. I said I can get information on almost anything they want, a bit of a brag on my part, I had no idea if I could or not. They asked me if I would give them anything I knew. "Sure, we work on the same team don't we?" I asked what it was they wanted and to give me a few days. I saw them sneer as I turned to leave. What is it with these people? My face clearly didn't fit, and it was time I proved to them I could do my job. I arrived back at my office, asked my secretary "Karen, we have a problem. I've promised two guys down the corridor information about a company, how much do we have, and how do we sort out the rubbish from the good stuff?" She looked at her screen, we had thirty thousand images of copied material regarding the company. "If you could print out, let's say, three thousand of the most useful stuff for them and throw in a few backside images if we have any". It's amazing how many people photocopy their private parts, for whatever reason. I guess sexting hadn't been invented yet. "No problem" she replied, confident her data system would work on its first test. It was done in no time, but we waited a few days to make it look like we had to work for the information. A few days later, I wasn't in the building but Karen delivered several boxes, about three thousand pages of information to their office. "Courtesy of Andy," she said, as she dumped the last box down on his desk. She left before he had a chance to say anything. A few days later, I got a phone call from him. "Andy this stuff is everything we need, how did you do this work, and so quickly? It's good stuff thank you". Finally, I had made my mark. So many times after that, people started coming to me asking if I had any information useful for whatever they were working on. So many times Karen and I could help. They started to question Karen to give up our secret, how did we have so much information and so quickly. She never did, nor did I. It was so simple, thinking always outside the established boxes, I developed different ways to achieve goals, in more efficient and less dangerous ways. Always with Karen right there for me, she was an incredible lady.

A few weeks later I had a call from "C". "I hear you are being very useful, well done. Meet me soon I have your first brief." I'd done it, I was becoming trusted and people began to talk to me, not as someone from the wrong side of the tracks. I was happy.

If you are in some doubt to the point of all the information gleaned from these photocopies it is this. Ask yourself what is the role of an MI6 Officer? The Secret Intelligence Service is the foreign intelligence service of the government of the United Kingdom, tasked mainly with the covert overseas collection and analysis of human intelligence (HUMINT) in support of the UK's national security. Agents are at the heart of what MI6 does.

Usually foreign nationals, they voluntarily work with us to provide secret intelligence that helps to keep the UK - and often the rest of the world – safe and secure. Our intelligence officers' major role is identifying, recruiting, and running these agents. Those copies of copies from so many companies, nearly all of whom export their business, provided invaluable information at base level, almost every photocopy gave us a name, address, and telephone numbers of people, of a potential that may be turned to help the UK. The stated priority roles of SIS are counter-terrorism, counter-proliferation, and supporting stability overseas to disrupt terrorism and other criminal activities

Around 2010 the photocopy machine hard drive problem was recognised by the machine manufacturers as a security risk. All manufacturers changed the method the images were stored. Nowadays these machines no longer store the images. Did that confine the SIS's capability to harvest such basic information? GCHQ centres around the country have grown, to more than replace my very simplistic method of the 70's. The technology is here now to do incredible things.

8. Morocco

One disadvantage I had as a new recruit was my absolute lack of experience abroad. By now there was a new "C" at MI6, Maurice Oldfield. A northerner, I liked him a lot. He had a much warmer character and treated me very fairly. He was identified in 1968 to the Russians as a prominent member of MI6 by the double agent Kim Philby. Oldfield was the main participant in restoring American confidence in the British intelligence service. He was knighted in 1975, and he retired in 1979, but he was called out of retirement by Prime Minister Margaret Thatcher to act as security coordinator in Northern Ireland. He stayed in that role from October 1979 to March 1980, when rumours of his hidden homosexuality forced his resignation. Already stricken with cancer, he died a year later.

Maurice offered me the opportunity to experience my first trip to foreign lands. I was given a brief for a small task in Morocco. Nothing heavy or too difficult, actually as it turned out it was more of a holiday. I arrived at Heathrow Airport and after checking in with Air Maroc to Tangier, I had no idea what to do next! I sat down on a seat watching everyone else. They seemed to go toward the back of the terminal for some reason, so I thought I'd better do the same. In those days security was almost nil, maybe a quick frisk down if you were unlucky. I cottoned on that I needed to find my flight on the screen and at the appropriate time, head to the gate. I arrived in Tangier a few hours later, the smells of spices and different scents immediately noticeable, and I loved it. I found my contact waiting in arrivals, who took me south to a small town called Asilah on the coast, about 45 minutes' drive away. I stayed at a place right by the sandy beach that stretched about 30 miles. I had a day to relax, I did some surfing and ate well in restaurants in town. Next day we took a drive further south to Rabat to the Royal Palace where King Hassan II had faced an attempted coup in 1972. The palace was a beautiful low complex, with gardens and opulence I'd never seen before. My job was to liaise with several people, one being a CIA agent, who was present to negotiate terms for secret US bases, and to pay rent directly to the King. The rent to be somewhere in the region of six hundred million US dollars. I had to set up a line of communication for shared intelligence with several agencies. There was some considerable corruption to clinch the deal. I passed information to the King about several corrupt officials, who were later sacked. Job done, I returned to Asilah hung around a few days enjoying new foods and the sun. My biggest mistake was not realising how strong the sun was this far south. Surfing and sunbathing I ended up with the most severe sunstroke. Shaking and vomiting most of two days it was a terrible experience I'd never repeat. As soon as I could move again I returned to Tangier and my flight home. Lessons learnt: how an airport works, how to eat couscous with one hand correctly, foreign sun can be dangerous.

9. In Love

After the successful Morocco trip, just before Christmas, Karen called me by telephone. "Hi Andy, are you coming to the company Christmas party?"

"I hadn't thought about it" I replied. I enjoyed parties, and indeed in those days I went to many among my group of friends. I wasn't good at dancing, and I rarely did, but they were always good fun.

"Can you come to the party please, it's always a good laugh, and it will be good to see my boss before Christmas"

"Well, I don't know anyone, but yes, it will be good to see you in an informal atmosphere for a change"

"Great, see you there, meet you at the bar, I drink gin and tonic if you're buying". She said cheekily.

"Of course, I wouldn't have it any other way". Call me old fashion, but I'd never let a girl buy her own drinks. It's how it was in those days.

On the evening of the party, I took a small overnight bag intending to sleep on one of the cots. There were rooms with single beds for staff to sleep on for those working late-night moments, which was quite often as officers and staff work with so many people in other countries. I left my bag in my office.

I wandered down to the common room where the party was warming up. No sign of Karen, so I sat alone at the bar and ordered myself a gin and tonic which I sipped slowly, I didn't want to get drunk too quickly.

About twenty minutes later Karen arrived, looking absolutely stunning, a few heads turned as she walked toward me at the bar. It was the first time I'd seen her out of secretarial dress code. She had an amazing dress sense that complimented a perfect figure. The nearest I could describe her would be a shorter Holly Willoughby, with a bit of Kelly Brook thrown in, both well know TV personalities in the UK. She was wearing a little black dress and matching heels, cut low enough at the front to reveal a very sexy cleavage. Oh my, she had boobs and legs to match. For the first time, I saw her with her hair down. I was very pleased that she chose to sit next to me at the bar, I bought her gin and tonic as requested. We sat and made small talk trying to avoid business matters. We chatted for about three drinks, occasionally interrupted by the odd guy coming up to ask her to dance, she refused them all. A few girls came to chat too, I didn't know any of them, but they inferred that I was becoming famous within SIS for the work I was doing. I didn't want to talk about any of it, so just smiled politely. One or two of them asked me to dance, I declined, because my dance technique was definitely "no dad" in style.

After our three drinks, I could see that Karen was getting into the party mood, and she said she would like to dance. I just don't do dancing, although I can manage a slow waltz or last dance. I told Karen to go enjoy herself, I'll look after our drinks. I'm a proper wallflower. She went to the dance-floor and danced with a few of the girls, she could move well too. A few of the guys tried to join her but she turned away each time, slowly making her way toward me. It seemed she was dancing for my benefit and pleasure, looking at me most of the time. She did have the kindest eyes and best smile. After about three songs she came back to the bar where I was still sat, complaining she was thirsty. I bought more drinks for us both. She asked if I ever danced, I told her I may try the slow dances when the DJ gets to the slow section. I was loosening up enough to start telling jokes and funny stories, to anyone that came to join us. It was a great evening, people let their hair down after the year of hard work. A slow song came on, and I finally plucked up the courage to ask Karen to dance with me, to my surprise she said yes! We held each other like old friends, I whispered a few corny words to her such as how beautiful she looked, and that I was the luckiest boss to have the best secretary in the whole building, to which she replied "What? Not the whole of London?" and then whispered, "I'm glad you came tonight, and I've dressed for you". This took me back a bit. Was this the drink talking? She was certainly the most attractive girl in the room, and a few guys were looking at me jealously for sure. "Well, thank you, you have dressed perfectly" not quite sure what to say next. I really am useless when it comes to girls. We danced close together until the song ended. We walked back to the bar holding hands. At the bar, Karen started, "Sorry Andy that wasn't very professional of me"

I replied, "It's fine, it is the first time I've enjoyed a dance, and I expect it was just the drink talking."

To which she replied looking into my eyes "No it's not", we looked at each other for a second or two. She then perked up, "Another drink? The evening hasn't finished yet" killing the moment completely.

We sat at the bar, had more drinks, had many laughs, she was very easy to get on with, if she wasn't my secretary I could have fallen in love with her, I probably had.

The last dance came and we held hands back to the dance floor, Karen rejecting requests from other guys on the way and holding my hand tighter, we had a very slow dance together. The evening ended and people were talking in groups and slowly drifting off. Karen asked me if I was travelling back to Leavesden, I said no I was planning on crashing on a cot. She suggested it may be more comfortable if I crashed at her flat, she would feel safer in my company on the train home that late at night. She lived one stop away on the London Underground at Elephant and Castle. It seemed a good idea, I wasn't going to argue.

Karen had a beautiful modern flat, bought for her by her father, a London Banker of some sort working for one of the banks I had stolen photocopy images from, but I didn't know that at the time. It was about 2 am by the time we arrived there. Not only did she have a perfect dress sense, but she also knew how to furnish a flat, it was a lovely place, painted in soft relaxing colours, the furnishings match well and it was easy to make myself at home, as she asked me to do. There were two bedrooms, to keep running costs down she rented the second bedroom to a colleague, one of the admin staff. We had no idea if she was home or not but we didn't keep particularly quiet other than the normal low voice one naturally uses late at night. I stood looking at the sofa, wondering how I was going to fold myself to sleep on it, as it was only a two-seater, while she made two cups of filtered coffee. Karen came into the lounge from the kitchen, placed the coffees on a low table next to the sofa and put some music on her record player. Sly & The Family Stone, Fresh album. The songs seemed quite mellow after the loud party music. We sat and chatted while drinking our coffees. When the music finished, she took the cups to the kitchen, came back into the lounge and declared she was going to bed. I asked if she had a blanket. "Andy, don't be silly, come with me." With that, she took my hand and led me into her bedroom. I was so slow with girls, I honestly didn't read the situation at all, I genuinely thought she was offering her sofa for the night.

In the morning, we woke at about eight, I opened my eyes to see her smiling at me. She gave me a morning kiss, got out of bed naked and went to the kitchen to make coffee. I wasn't quite sure what had happened, she was seven years older than me, yet, at work my subordinate. She came back to bed with a coffee each. It was an awkward moment for me. Did this mean we were together now? Karen broke the silence. "You know we can't be together. Fraternising at work is severely frowned upon". My heart sank, I knew I had fallen in love with her. "I'm sorry it wasn't very professional of me to lead you on." She added.

"So, I'm a one night stand? Is that what you are saying?" I questioned,

"Not at all, I've loved you from the first day I met you, it was love at first sight".

"Me too" I replied, I could not understand why she fell in love with me, the boy from nowhere.

"I will be transferred to another department if they find out. I don't want that. I love working for you".

"Why?" I asked, "Why am I so different from any of the others?"

"Because you treat me like an equal, you never ask me to do anything you are not prepared to do yourself, you are polite and kind. Unlike some of those private school idiots. They treat women like a lesser being, something to show off and abuse. Plus, I have to admit, you are very handsome too. But, I need to remain professional, I love my job, I do not want to lose it" I blushed, no one had ever said such nice words to me, I'd not had any girlfriends at school or since until now if that is the label I should give her. I could see her point though, tough as it was, there were security implications prohibiting staff from getting so close. I was prepared to quit my job today if it meant we could be together. I left for home around midday after a delightful morning together.

Not being able to be with Karen was difficult for me to cope with. I had fallen in love with her, I knew she liked me too, yet, we could not be together openly. To compensate, I spent the next few years enjoying all kinds of sports. I started windsurfing, a guy at Rickmansworth Aquadrome was giving lessons and I took to it straight away. I'd done some dinghy sailing with my father which made the principles of windsurfing easier. My Dad and I sailed an Enterprise dinghy at a club at Henley-on-Thames. Later he bought a kit, a self-build Mirror dingy. I helped to build the boat with him which was fun. The windsurfing took off well, my instructor, I and a few others formed the windsurfing section at Rickmansworth Sailing Club, Troy Lake, West Hyde.

Fig. 2. The author water-skiing at Willen Lake, Milton Keynes.

I'm not sure if the windsurfing section still exists today. I also bought a Plancraft Stingray speedboat and learnt to water ski. I often went with friends to Swanage, Poole or Willen Lake near Milton Keynes for weekends water-skiing. I also had a go at parachuting at Sibson Airfield near Peterborough. In those days, we were trained to jump a solo static-line jump, I don't think tandem jumping had been invented yet. I spent a day learning how to do Parachute Landing Falls, or PLF's, which meant a lot of running and jumping off various heights forward, sideways, and backwards. The beginner group progressed by the end of a weekend to jumping out of a mock aircraft door on a short zip-line to practice every kind of PLF. Finally, we had to jump from the just below the roof of the hanger on a fan-line, which was just a line wound around a winch on a fan. The fan provided resistance to slow your fall slightly. Some of the group dropped out at this point, they couldn't jump from so high. I completed the weekend course but the weather was too bad to try an actual jump from the club's Pilatus Porter aircraft. I went back a few weeks later and did my first static line jump, I did find the landing harder than I had been trained for, but it was not too painful. I was the only person in my jump group that landed on target, a circle of gravel in the field. Work and other matters prevented me from continuing with parachuting. I had plenty of other sports I preferred. However, I also had a love for flying, I'd had a go at trial flights in gliders and small aircraft, so I decided to try for my Private Pilot's Licence (PPL). In those days learning to fly was far easier and cheaper than today. I joined a Flying Club for Servicemen and women and affiliated civilians. I started flying a Cessna 172 from RAF Halton near Aylesbury, Buckinghamshire. Unfortunately, after starting the course, my instructor fell ill and died, my lessons were cancelled, my workload increased, one thing led to another and I never completed the course or achieved my PPL.

I also pushed loads of weights in the gym and attended men's keep-fit classes. All of this was my way to distract myself in my spare time from thinking about girls, especially Karen, as well as to keep me very fit. Karen and I kept our relationship professional and did not see each other outside of work. The Christmas party over-night stay, however, did become a tradition, one that we both enjoyed.

10. Emails

As computer systems became the norm and communicating on networks developed. It occurred to me this should be a quicker and simpler method for Karen and me to utilise. By now I had a computer at home and seldom went to London. My meetings were mostly outside the building in randomly selected venues, safer and more secure for private conversations. Many private clubs in the city became known meeting places, London seemed to be the spy centre of the world. As this list shows just a few well-known locations, anyone wanting to avoid being suspected a spy avoided Century House, as I did.

Tin and Stone Bridge, St James's Park. Between Buckingham Palace and the ministries of Whitehall, this location was used by British Intelligence (and may still be) as a meeting point with all manner of people. New recruits were often met here, the location instilling a sense of pride and importance in those about to embark upon a career in the Service.

In and Out Club, Piccadilly. A recruiting venue for MI5 and MI6, this address was also used in correspondence found on a dead British officer who was deliberately dropped into the sea off Spain by MI6 during the Second World War. This deception operation tricked the Nazis into believing the Normandy invasion force would land elsewhere. It is still a private members' club.

Boodle's, 28 St James's Street. This London club played host to many famous MI6 officers. It was an ideal location for events and recruiting. Ian Fleming, the creator of

James Bond and an MI6 man, was a frequent visitor during his days in the city.

White's, 37-38 St James's Street. Another popular meeting point and recruitment venue, this members' club was used for decades by MI5 and MI6.

St Ermin's Hotel, Caxton Street. Used by MI6 as a Second World War operational centre. Parts of the building were also occupied by operatives from Britain's wartime Special Operations Executive (SOE).

The Tophams Hotel, 26 Ebury Court. A venue used extensively in the Second World War by officers from MI6 and the SOE. The SOE expanded greatly during the war, and this location hosted many foreign nationals who signed up to become agents.

Leconfield House, Mayfair. This building became MI5's headquarters in early 1945. Its original structure had specially designed windows to support machine guns – just in case the Germans ever reached London. Also, inside was an MI5 bar called the "Pig and Eye". Many famous names from the Service drank here, including Peter Wright, author of one of the world's most famous espionage books, Spycatcher.

18 Carlyle Square, Chelsea. This address was once home to one of Britain's most infamous spy figures, Kim Philby. Philby was an MI6 officer who became a top KGB spy, betraying many secrets to Moscow in the 1950s.

Brompton Oratory, Knightsbridge. At the beginning of the Cold War, the KGB planted dozens of agents in London. One of the most famous locations for exchanging information was this building. Packages were secreted behind pillars and collected by agents.

Holy Trinity Church, Knightsbridge. Just behind Brompton Oratory. It too was used by KGB agents as a "dead letter drop" – a form of spy tradecraft that involves the deposit and collection of secret materials. In this case, packages were tucked behind the statue.

Cafe Daquise, near South Kensington Tube. The cafe, which has been modernised, is a short walk from Brompton Oratory and was used by the KGB and other spy agencies for years. Perhaps two of its most famous clients were Christine Keeler, a London socialite in the Sixties, and John Profumo, Britain's Secretary of State for War. Unbeknown to Profumo, Keeler's other lover happened to be a top Soviet diplomat – Eugene Ivanov. The 1963 liaison became known as "The Profumo Affair" – a scandal that almost brought down the British Government.

Millennium Hotel, Knightsbridge. In 2006 this hotel unknowingly played host to a small party of Russians, at least one with a deadly agenda. Among the group, former KGB man and exile Alexander Litvinenko ordered a cup of green tea. Within days he fell critically ill, suffering from the effects of deadly Polonium-210, a particle of which had been slipped into his tea.

The list goes on! For me London was not the place to be, in my opinion, why would I want to be seen meeting and hanging around in these places. Business could be done outside the city, and that is how I operated. Despite how it seems, working for SIS is not a very dangerous job. Normally what happens in the services is that the risks are run by the agents – the people I and the other Officers recruit. For example, if I wanted to find out about a country's nuclear production tomorrow I couldn't wander into a facility in that country, no matter how good my cover was. But I can recruit a scientist who is already there. Of course, if the operation goes tits up, the person who is usually going to suffer is the agent, not me.

A meeting was called to consider the new communications systems now coming into use with the Internet readily available. The problem with the Internet, and even more so telephones, is that so many countries are intercepting them. The UK, USA, China, Russia, Israel, Saudi Arabia, are only part of an astonishingly long list of countries that listen to our every conversation by landline, Internet or mobile phone today.

The Government Communications Headquarters (GCHQ) is an intelligence and security organisation responsible for providing signals intelligence (SIGINT) and information to the government and armed forces of the United Kingdom. Now based in the suburbs of Cheltenham, GCHQ is the responsibility of the country's Secretary of State for Foreign and Commonwealth Affairs, but it is not a part of the Foreign Office and its Director ranks as a Permanent Secretary.

GCHQ was originally established after the First World War as the Government Code and Cypher School (GC&CS) and was known under that name until 1946. During the Second World War, it was located at Bletchley Park, where it was responsible for breaking of the German Enigma codes. There are two main components of the GCHQ, the Composite Signals Organisation (CSO), which is responsible for gathering information, and the National Cyber Security Centre (NCSC), which is responsible for securing the UK's own communications. The Joint Technical Language Service

(JTLS) is a small department and cross-government resource responsible for mainly technical language support and translation and interpreting services across government departments. It is co-located with GCHQ for administrative purposes.

Morwenstow is another Signals intelligence (SIGINT) centre in the UK, of which there are several. SIGINT is intelligence-gathering by interception of signals, whether communications between people (communications intelligence, COMINT) or from electronic signals not directly used in communication (electronic intelligence, ELINT). In 2013, GCHQ received considerable media attention when the former National Security Agency contractor Edward Snowden revealed that the agency was in the process of collecting all online and telephone data in the UK via the Tempora programme. Snowden's revelations began a spate of ongoing disclosures of global surveillance. The Guardian newspaper was then forced to destroy all incriminating files given to them by Snowden because of the threats of lawsuits from the UK Government. Documents Snowden acquired claimed that data collected by the Tempora program is shared with the National Security Agency of the United States.

The "Email Problem" meeting took place with various staff from different departments within SIS, to establish secure methods of communicating. I was invited for reasons unknown, maybe my now widely known ability to always come up with a different line of thought was considered a useful addition. The discussions were way above my skill-level and eventually came around to emails. We were warned that all emails were being intercepted around the world and that it was definitely not a good idea to use the system to communicate privately. I spoke up without even thinking about it. "Well then", I said, "don't send your email". Asked what I meant I continued, "I can't see any problem in writing a draft email, and just not send it, leave it as a draft". A few of those present saw what I was getting at. "When you have an email account you first need an email address that can be a kind of password code, for instance, my email maybe blue-musketeer@fco.gov.uk, the blue-musketeer part being a partial security code, you'd need to be told my email address to contact me. I could write an email and leave it as a draft. Anyone wanting to read my email draft would also need to know how to enter my account, which also needs a pin or code. So this sets up a two-password entry system. Once into my account, you can read my email draft. The draft email has not been sent, therefore, no one can intercept it." I said it on the spur of the moment, without thinking about what I had said. The IT people present thought about it and confirmed yes it was true. An unsent email draft could not be intercepted provided the Internet Protocol (IP) address was varied or hidden. It was possible to use a virtual private network (VPN) which is a technology that creates a safe and encrypted connection over a less secure network, such as the Internet. Most of us used a VPN as standard in the SIS.

The idea came to me at that moment, I didn't know if it would work, but the technical boffins confirmed that it was a reasonably safe method of writing messages, so long as the email address and account code were kept secret between the two or group of people communicating with each other. My 'out of the box' way of thinking had come up with a method for low-security emails to be utilised. Unfortunately, it did leave the technical teams a little red-faced, but a few of all those present saw the funny side of it. Sometimes simple things are the best. The method was passed and emails were permitted in draft form, and a method was devised to pass the two bits of information necessary for it to work safely.

11. In another Love

November 1977, my friend Martin and I were together one day and we went to invite his girlfriend to his 21st birthday party. Martin's girlfriend (another Karen for ease of writing I'll call her Karen G.), wasn't at home at the time, but her sister was. Janine was 17 years old, we didn't know Karen G. had a sister, quite a looker, so we invited her too. I liked her immediately and Janine and I started seeing each other as friends. At last, I could put the pain of separation from Karen my secretary behind me and move forward in a new relationship.

Martin a Royal Marine was helpful, as kids, we had lived in the same street in Maple Cross. Because of an injury to his leg in training, he was posted to Combined Task Force (CTF) 345 at Northwood, then had a posting at the Ministry of Defence (MOD) London, which proved useful to me in 1982 during the Falklands War, I'd sometimes get information before anyone at MI6. One such piece of information was regarding the death of another friend from Rickmansworth Grammar School, Laurence Watts, we affectionately knew him as Polly Watts due to his rather parrot size and shaped nose.

Corporal Laurence WATTS, 42 Commando, Royal Marines. Date of Death: 11/12 June 1982. During the attack on Mount Harriett, as a section commander, he was clearing an Argentinian bivouac whose occupants were armed with rifles. He was so close he was actually pushing a rifle away when he was shot in the neck. He fell back, bleeding badly, but returned to the attack, firing his rifle, only to be shot again, the bullet passing through his radio set and then through his heart.

Martin informed me of Polly's death because it was highly likely I may bump into his younger brother, a Captain in the Marines. It would have been embarrassing if I had said anything before his family had been informed officially.

Janine was a lovely girl, quite pretty, attractive, very funny and intelligent. Short brown hair, attractive figure, curvy in all the right places. She rode a motorbike, on which she became quite noticeable wearing her black flocked helmet. I had it flocked for her as the company next to the printing works did that kind of thing. I had no idea if it was legal. Her hobby was diving, she was a member of the Watford Diving Club. We spent several weekends at Swanage on club dives, where, while she was diving with her sister and club mates, I'd spend time ashore with the wives. I have learnt to dive since, but it's not a sport I enjoy.

We spent all our spare time together, as young lovers should. Always going places and to parties, It didn't take long for me to pluck up the courage to ask her to marry me, and in 1979 I did just that. Thinking about it now, the way I proposed was unbelievably corny. I bought her a microwave for Christmas, unpacked it carefully, and fixed the ring inside the microwave onto the plate, re-packed it carefully good as new. I can't think what she must have thought about such an awful impersonal present, but it didn't take her long to find the ring inside. Thankfully, she said yes. She was 19 and I 24.

We bought a small one-bedroom ground floor flat 137 Gladstone Road, Watford. It was so small I had to post my windsurfer mast through the front window into the lounge, as it was too long to get through any door and round the corridor to store somewhere. I couldn't keep it outside as there was nowhere safe to keep the mast and board and the flat had no garden.

The flat backed onto the Watford main railway line, it was difficult to sleep at night with the noise of trains, and at about 3 am a few times a week the nuclear waste train would creep by at dead slow pace taking forever to pass.

Our wedding plans began to get organised. The church was booked, cars, wedding reception venue and invites sent out. One day, out of the blue, Janine wouldn't answer her phone. I didn't know what was going on. A few days later she broke the news to me that she didn't feel ready to marry, she was too young. I was absolutely heartbroken. I took a few days off work to try to sort things out, I didn't say why I needed the time off. Nobody could explain to me what had happened, the wedding plans had to be cancelled. I went into a deep depression, alone in the flat we had bought together.

After a few days, my ever-faithful secretary telephoned, it was good to hear a kind voice again. People were wondering in London if I was safe. I had never disappeared without the knowledge of my masters in London. She asked if it would be ok for her and John my former mentor to come round, I reluctantly agreed, saying I wasn't good company, but I knew I had to snap out of my solitary depression. Karen arrived alone, John had been called away at the last minute. I had just been dumped by one girl I loved and here was another beautiful girl that I couldn't get closer to either. She tried so hard to make me feel good. She was so sweet, she made me cups of tea, and stayed with me for longer than she needed to. We sat on the sofa watching TV drinking tea, she was being a good friend as always. Occasionally we talked about work, but nothing heavy, we just nattered about what was going on. She was just a good friend and the only one that turned up to see me, out of all of my group of friends. She offered to help cancel the wedding arrangements, but my parents had that in hand. It wasn't clear to me if she could help, but at the end of the day, she showed she was a good friend as well as being fantastic at her job. I couldn't have asked any more from her, all she did was show kindness and genuine concern, sat with me for hours and hours, but the reality was, it just hurt more that two girls I loved so much did not, or could not, want me.

I didn't see Janine ever again. Until about 2008. She found me on Facebook. She sent me a message. "Hello, do you remember me?"

How could I not? Her second question was: "Do you forgive me?"

I replied "Of course, there is nothing to forgive", unsure of her motive, I didn't want to give her any idea that she had damaged me deeply. I looked into her history, saw how badly it had gone for her after we parted. Divorced with two children, Janine had a lot of personal problems. Her life didn't look good at all. Time had almost healed my wounds, but unfortunately, my bitterness was quite deep, my thoughts at that moment were quite bitter, "yeah, you got what you deserved", I thought to myself. But now, I think differently. Everyone makes choices for a reason, you cannot go through life thinking about how life *might* have been. If it goes well, good for you. If it goes wrong, learn the lesson, pick yourself up, dust yourself down and try something else. Janine and I had a great time together and she has given me many great memories that will last my lifetime. We now text each other occasionally, I no longer feel any animosity toward her, and I thank her for finding me again, even though we have never met.

12. Love And Marriage

1982 I met Julie at a friend's wedding. Jo and Sue had invited me to their wedding in May 1982. Jo was the friend at school that cut his head and fell from the first floor as we were trying to enter the school one early morning. A large group of friends were going to the wedding and I agreed to take a girl I knew, Michelle, in my car. Michelle liked me but I felt she wasn't my type. But we were friends, there wasn't a reason not to be, she was a pleasant person. The wedding reception in the evening was at Moor Park Golf Course near Rickmansworth. The clubhouse is a beautiful mansion house in the grounds of the golf course. It was a great event, entertaining speeches, with good food, and drink. In the evening there was music and dancing. One of Michelle's friends, Julie, spent most of the time with Michelle and me. I had met Julie before, she had come with Michelle to the Half-Way House pub, Mill End, just outside Rickmansworth a few times, where our group of friends met most weeks. We got on well that night too. Julie didn't have a lift home, so I offered to take her back to Croxley Green in my car at the end of the evening. As she got out of my car, we arranged to see each other again sometime soon. We started to date, at first I didn't think she was my type and wasn't sure if we should get any closer, maybe just remain friends. But Julie persisted and we became boyfriend and girlfriend soon after. A few years later I proposed to her. Ever aware that I had been dumped at that point in my relationship with Janine, I didn't really want that kind of hurt again, so I was a little wary of the idea. We rented a flat together, which was a nice, but fairly old flat in Moor Lane Crossing, just on the edge of Croxley Moor. In the summer it was nice living next to the moor, we'd go for barbeques by the river Gade that ran through the moor and parallel to the Grand Union canal. In the winter though, it was cold. Our heating was from a single open fire in the lounge. One winter it was so cold our toothpaste froze in the bathroom. We finally married at All Saints Church, Croxley Green. Our wedding reception was at the Watersmeet centre in Rickmansworth. We honeymooned in Padstow, Cornwall. Not long after, we bought a house together in Rowland Way, Aylesbury, Buckinghamshire. An ever-growing dormitory town, the town centre was an old market town, around its perimeter housing estate after housing estate expanded and grew. Most people that lived there commuted into London or Oxford. Our first daughter Joanne was born in July 1986 at the John Radcliff Hospital, Oxford.

For five years life was good for us at Aylesbury, but the town had little entertainment. Julie worked as a nurse, I commuted every day to work. I kept my real work from Julie, I don't know why it was just easier not to say anything to her. My thinking at the time was, how could I tell her that I was a spy? Imagine, you start going out with someone and they break the news to you that they are a spy, yeh that works. I'd just be accused of being a liar and fantasist.

She saw me leave for work in the company van belonging to the printing company. In reality, she had no idea where I was going. If I needed to go away for some time, I would tell her I was going sailing. I had a love for yachts as well as my speed boat and would go on sailing courses to complete my Day Skipper and Coastal Skipper certificates. These courses were attained by completing not only theory courses but many practical hours sailing were needed to qualify. This provided a good cover story. Life was good with Julie, we had fun, worked hard and she tolerated me being absent from home with no question. Life with her was easy, it may have been much harder if I had been with someone less tolerant of me disappearing every now and then. I never felt any guilt for always lying to her about my job and where I was working. I felt my job was too important for guilt, maybe I should have treated her differently, who knows, it was just how it was and seemed right for me at the time.

13. The Philippines.

Back at work and slowly regaining my dignity after the embarrassing cancellation of my wedding, I resumed my activities as the job demanded. I had minor roles in several major international stories. I can't claim these were my sole responsibility, however, I was asked by various officers and other characters to assist when needed. I only mention these operations here as they indicate the level of trust I had attained with the controllers of these operations.

I was given the Philippines as my main brief. Ferdinand Marcos (1917 - 1989) was a Filipino politician and kleptocrat. He was the tenth President of the Philippines from 1965 to 1986. A leading member of the far-right New Society Movement, he ruled as a dictator under martial law from 1972 until 1981. His regime was infamous for its corruption, extravagance, and brutality. Marcos claimed an active part in World War II, including fighting alongside the Americans in the Bataan Death March and being the "most decorated war hero in the Philippines". A number of his claims were found to be false and the United States Army documents described Marcos's wartime claims as "fraudulent" and "absurd". There began a pattern of loan-funded spending which the Marcos administration would continue until he was deposed in 1986, resulting in economic instability that is still being felt today, with debts that experts say the Philippines will have to keep paying well into 2025. Marcos constantly sought American approval. For years, though he abused human rights and, with his wife, Imelda, plundered the country of billions of dollars, the

United States tolerated him for the sake of its Philippine bases. American officials supported Marcos - until August 1983, the day Cory Aquino's husband, Benigno, was assassinated at Manila airport (now Ninoy Aquino airport) as he returned from American exile to challenge Marcos. The American Government now foresaw the collapse of the Marcos regime amid an eroding Philippine economy and a spreading Communist insurgency. Marcos, formerly guarantor of the American bases, was now placing them in jeopardy.

Marcos is known to have used false flag operations as a pretext for martial law. There were a series of deadly bombings, and the CIA privately stated that Marcos was responsible for at least one of them. I and the CIA were also almost certain that none of the bombings were perpetrated by Communists as Marcos claimed. Intelligence declassified documents contained further evidence implicating Marcos, provided by a mole within the Philippine army.

I was case-officer and controller to seven agents in Manila, all of which provided me with an incredible amount of information of every type. I knew almost every move Marcos made, sometimes even before he made them. One agent having access to his appointment book. After Marcos went into exile to Hawaii, taking with him on two planes not only his closest allies, but also loaded with loot, 23 wooden crates, 12 suitcases and bags, and various boxes, whose contents included enough clothes to fill 67 racks, 413 pieces of jewellery, 24 gold bricks, inscribed "To my husband on our 24th anniversary", and more than 27 million Philippine pesos in freshly printed notes. The jewellery included 70 pairs of jewel-studded cuff-links, an ivory statue of the infant Jesus with a silver mantle and a diamond necklace. The total value of these items was estimated at $15 million. Meanwhile, when protesters stormed Malacañang Palace in Manila, shortly after Marcos's departure, it was famously discovered that Imelda had left behind over 2,700 pairs of shoes in her closet.

There were massive protests and unrest, but only within Manila, in the provinces and islands it remained relatively calm. Some of my agents inside the Marcos circle left behind needed to flee also, some moved to Mindanao Island, about 500 miles south, where it was thought to be somewhat safer with none of the unrest seen in Manila.

I had personally started to mistrust the Americans also. For many reasons, I saw how America could not be trusted, as a so-called, partner. On several occasions promises were broken, help was not forthcoming either overt or covert. My view was not the official view however, I drew my opinions from my own personal experience.

14. Chris Curwen And Oleg Gordievsky

Christopher Curwen was Head of the Secret Intelligence Service (MI6) from 1985 to 1989. Curwen was awarded CMG in 1982 and KCMG in 1986. It was under Chris that the Service brought off one of its most spectacular coups, the extraction from Moscow of the agent Oleg Gordievsky. I cannot claim for one moment to have played any major part in the Gordievsky story, but the tiniest role that I did, does give me a modest claim to that historic event.

In brief, Gordievsky was recruited by SIS in 1974, Gordievsky was the British Secret Intelligence Service star source inside the KGB. He had provided valuable reports at a critical time in the Cold War, a period in which paranoia at the Kremlin had become so bad that the NATO 1983 Able Archer exercise had been misinterpreted in Moscow as a possible cover for a surprise attack on the Soviet Bloc. As well as producing enormous quantities of documents from the KGB station in London, where he had been posted in June 1982, Gordievsky had identified KGB personnel in British and Scandinavian departments and had shed light on dozens of past cases.

Gordievsky was summoned back to Moscow from London, supposedly for consultations. On his arrival, he realised that his apartment had been searched, and when he reached First Chief Directorate (FCD), headquarters he was accused of being a spy. When he denied it, his interrogators used drugs in an unsuccessful attempt to extract a confession, and he concluded that, although the KGB had been tipped off to his dual role, there was insufficient evidence to justify an arrest. Although he remained under constant surveillance, in late July, Gordievsky was able to shake off his watchers while jogging in a park and sent an emergency signal to SIS requesting a rescue

His escape from Moscow is one of the greatest spy stories in history, there are books and TV films about it. The bravery of Viscount Asquith, MI6 Moscow station commander who drove the escape car and the coolness of his female assistant when she dropped a dirty nappy from their Saab car when they were stopped by a patrol, was, in my mind one of the greatest spy actions. The nappy distracted the sniffer dog from detecting Gordievsky hiding in the boot of the car.

Gordievsky was briefly accommodated at a country safe house in the Midlands, where Curwen visited him, and then at Fort Monckton, Gosport, where he underwent an 80-day debriefing conducted by SIS's principal Kremlinologist. Among Gordievsky's other visitors was the US Director of Central Intelligence, who was flown down to the fort for a lunch hosted by Curwen, a celebration of one of SIS's most impressive post-war coups. In all Gordievsky was spying for the UK for 10 years.

I was asked by Curwen to collect Gordievsky from the country safe house in the Midlands and drive him to Fort Monkton. I am able to say that I talked with and sat beside Gordievsky on that journey for a few hours.

Although Gordievsky's safe escape was a source of great pride for Curwen and his staff, there remained considerable concern about precisely how the agent had been compromised. One possibility was that, after so many setbacks, the KGB had worked out for itself that a mole had been at work within the organisation. Had Gordievsky's dual role somehow been leaked by a mole? It is now that I started to have suspicions that there may be a dangerous leak in MI6. A leak that later in my career will have near-fatal consequences for me.

15. The Falklands War

In April 1982 Argentina invaded the Falkland Islands. Argentina had claimed sovereignty over the islands for many years and their ruling military junta did not believe that Britain would attempt to regain the islands by force. Britain, under the leadership of Margaret Thatcher, undertook the extraordinary feat of assembling and sending a task force of warships and rapidly refitted merchant ships to the Falklands. Despite the huge distance involved, the Falklands were 8,000 miles away in the South Atlantic, the task force reached the Falklands in early May. On 2nd May, the Royal Navy submarine HMS Conqueror sank the Argentinian cruiser General Belgrano, with the loss of over 300 of her crew. After this incident, Argentinian ships remained in port. However, the Argentinian air force still posed a significant threat. The Royal Navy lost several warships to attacks by Argentinian aircraft. Super Étendard warplanes were armed with missiles most significantly of which was the French manufactured Exocet missile. In May 1982 these Exocet missiles were used to strike Britain's HMS Sheffield and Atlantic Conveyor, with the loss of 32 British lives, near panic ensued in London. It became imperative to stop further British losses due to Exocet missiles.

At the start of the conflict, France's president, Francois Mitterrand, had come to Britain's aid by declaring an embargo on French arms sales and assistance to Argentina. He also gave permission for the Falklands-bound British fleet to use French port facilities in West Africa, as well as providing London with detailed information about planes and weaponry his country had sold to Argentina. Paris also co-operated with extensive British efforts to stop Argentina acquiring any more Exocets on the world's arms market. There was, however, a feeling, if not proof that France was acting in a somewhat duplicitous way. It came to my knowledge that there was a French technical team in Argentina assisting the air force to fix some missile launchers, three of the launchers had failed to work. Thanks to the work of the French, the Argentinians were able to launch Exocets at British forces from three previously faulty missile launchers.

The British knew that Argentina had only five Exocet missiles. Plans were put into place to destroy the three remaining Exocet missiles which Argentina still had in its possession. Operation Mikado was the code name of the military plan by the United Kingdom to use Special Air Service (SAS) troops to attack the home base of Argentina's five Étendard strike fighters at Río Grande, Tierra del Fuego. The man in charge of the planning was Brigadier Peter de la Billière, then Head of the SAS. He proposed an operation similar to Operation Entebbe, which consisted of landing 55 SAS soldiers in two Lockheed C-130 Hercules aircraft directly on the runway at Rio Grande. The aim of the operation was to destroy the three remaining Exocet missiles that Argentina had in its possession, and the aircraft that carried them, and to kill the pilots in their quarters.

Operation Plum Duff, a preliminary reconnaissance mission on Río Grande, was launched from HMS Invincible on the night of 17/18 May, as a prelude to the attack. The operation consisted of transporting by helicopter a small SAS team to the Argentine side of Tierra del Fuego. The team would then march to the Rio Grande air base and proceed to set up an observation post to collect intelligence on the base before the main assault. The helicopter would be operating to the limits of its range, which made some call it a suicide mission. During the flight it was necessary to divert to avoid a drilling rig adding twenty minutes to the flight and, nearing the coast, dense fog had reduced visibility forcing the pilot to land. The helicopter was destroyed and the pilots after several nights walk were picked up by Chilean Military and returned to British Officials. Operation Plum Duff was abandoned. The Chilean armed forces had a long and close relationship with Britain and the Chilean junta kept quiet.

What could the British do about the Exocet threat? MI6 was working on the problem in the background and it fell to us to submit plans. John Nott, the Secretary of State for Defence at the time of the war authorised an operation, some have described it as out of a James Bond movie. MI6 launched an elaborate deception operation designed to convince the Argentinians that arms dealers were buying Exocets on their behalf when the real aim was to ensure no missiles were ever delivered, or, using technical advice supplied by the French, render them inoperable before reaching Buenos Aires. It would reassure the Task Force once the five missiles in Argentine possession had been launched there could be no further Exocet attack.

The operation masterminded by an SIS Officer known as Anthony Baynham was to monitor the arms market using Tony Divall a former Royal Marine NCO who had an established an arms dealing business in Germany. Divall had previous associations with SIS. £16million of government money had been deposited in a bank to use for letters of credit. John Dutcher, an American dealer, had been employed by Divall to offer his services to Carlos Corti, a major personality in the Paris arms supply effort for Argentina. Corti had diplomatic status, he had already lost over $6million to a fraudulent deal in Holland. A deal was identified for twenty missiles at $1.5million each. Buyers in such deals generally show money is available through a letter of credit, while sellers deposit a performance bond. No performance bond was produced. Following furious negotiations, it was suggested that a meeting was set up at Orly Airport France. Nothing was brought to the meeting, but a substantial advance payment was demanded from the Argentinian. In a somewhat dramatic move, the buyers stormed out as no missiles were available for inspection by an expert on Corti's side either. The deal never went through, Corti was withdrawn by the Argentine Government before the fake deal went any further and more money was lost. From now on the British could identify and monitor all the Argentines players and their associates that were operating to effect a black market purchase. Arms deals could now be infiltrated. No Exocet missiles ever became available on the black market again during the conflict.

Another direction arms were reaching Argentina was through Israel. The Israeli Prime Minister Menachem Begin agreed to help Argentina during the Falklands War as revenge for Britain's crackdown on the Jewish Irgun during the British mandate of Palestine until the formation of Israel. Israel armed Argentina's military dictatorship with air-to-air missiles, fuel tanks for fighter bombers, gas masks and missile radar alert systems. Many components of these weapons were American. There is a law that prohibits the sale of any military component to third parties without the authorisation of the White House. Here again, my miss-trust of the Americans grew deeper. If the United States hadn't turned a blind eye, it would have been impossible for Israel to send such a large amount of weapons.

I was a conduit for several agents in France, Italy, and Chile and fed information to the Ministry of Defence and the Foreign Office. One SIS agent lost his life, after being part of the covert operations during the Falkland Island conflict. Probably due to a traitor within SIS itself. Mistrust of Americans and Israelis and my suspicions of a 'mole' regarding Gordievsky's position being compromised to the Russians were being cemented. One important point to stress is normally SIS Officers do not involve themselves directly with operations in the country of operation, they are the controllers of the agents that do the dangerous work. Often the simplest of information can be invaluable. It is not always necessary for an agent to infiltrate a government or organisation, a simple agent can be invaluable by supplying information in the form of observation. Movement of traffic from an army base or watching a coastline around a naval base can be most helpful. One of the most effective ways to gather data and information about the enemy (or potential enemy) is by infiltrating the enemy's ranks. This is the job of the spy. Spies can return information concerning the size and strength of enemy forces. They can also find dissidents within the enemy's forces and influence them to defect also.

My position was about to change. Due to the loss of an agent in-country (another suspicious loss in my mind, which would later prove to be true), it became an urgent matter that someone should perfect their Spanish and become faultless with a fake identity. There was no time to recruit a new agent. I was asked to move into character and country and undertake a mission in one of the most dangerous countries of the time, Angola.

16. Invitation To Angola

At the beginning of December 1988, I received a message, via Karen, to attend a meeting with 'C', Chris Curwen. The meeting was to be at the Reform Club, London. It is a private members club on the south side of Pall Mall, in what is often called London's Clubland. I arrived in London with little idea as to what the meeting was going to be regarding, this was nothing unusual, sometimes things needed to be that way. I caught a train from Amersham having driven from Aylesbury and soon arrived at Piccadilly Underground Station. In Pall Mall, I found the club with some difficulty as it only had a small name plaque on the pillar at the bottom of the steps up to the entrance, I was looking for a larger sign over the door, the club seemed very discreet.

Inside the entrance, the space was surprisingly light. It had a beautiful rectangular shaped glass-domed roof, letting in plenty of light over the reception area. With columns supporting a balcony around the entire first floor, reminding me of the Riad I stayed at in Morocco, but this building was far more opulent. The floor was a white patterned mosaic with an Octagon at its centre. To the right was the reception desk, where, when I enquired, I was told I was expected. I was led up the wide stairs opposite the front door to the first floor and led around the balcony to a private room on the left. I could tell this was going to be a special meeting, it was different from any of the other meeting rooms I had attended. The room was panelled in a light coloured wood, the furnishings were matching with red material making the room have a very rich feel but with a comfortable aura to it. 'C' was sitting at the head of a rectangular table in the centre of the room with eight chairs around it. I was invited to sit at a seat opposite 'C' and asked whether I would like a drink. I ordered a pot of my favourite English Breakfast tea. Seated at the table were two other people I knew, Jean a linguist expert, Max an assistant to 'C'. Sat on 'Chris's right was another guy I hadn't met before, but he had a file in front of him in a folder, I couldn't read the label on the front of the file from where I sat at the far end of the table. It all looked a little intimidating, my initial thoughts on seeing this collection of people was that I was here for a disciplinary of some kind, but I knew I hadn't done anything wrong (ignoring the fact I'd spent years stealing photocopies from companies across England), so I had nothing to be alarmed at. 'C' spoke first and got straight to the point.

"Hello Andy, I trust you found your journey trouble-free today, thank you for coming. We have a situation, and I think you will be suitable for the job." He went on to explain who the guy on his right was. "I will introduce you to Roger. Roger has interests concerning the United Nations and has assets inside working for us. He runs his own section at Century House specialising exclusively with the UN. I need you to prepare for a trip abroad. Roger thinks that you will be perfect for this job simply because we have very little time, and you fit the profile of the position I want you to fill."

"Ok" responded a little puzzled.

Roger started to speak, "We have a situation. One of our agents has been compromised and we would like you to take his place. As you know there has been war in Angola for many years, it is <u>not</u> a pleasant country." Emphasising the 'not' in a high pitch tone, which seemed to surprise even himself. He went on.

"The war is a little complicated, you may know there are quite a few factions involved. The MPLA supported by the Cubans. UNITA with the support of the South African government. The United States sided with the FNLA." he continued after taking a breath, "In August 1975, it was UNITA that formally declared war on the MPLA, after the withdrawal of Portugal, who ran Angola as a colony since 1575. I would say is the simplest way to describe the situation."

"Goodness, sounds complicated, are you sure a simple soul like me can handle such complexity?" I asked.

Roger continued. "The point is, we need someone to replace our agent. A complex international diplomatic process aimed at achieving peace and stability in the region has resulted in agreements on all sides of the implementation of Security Council resolution 626 (1988), aimed at verifying the withdrawal of Cuban troops from Angola. Under the agreement, the United Nations Angola Verification Mission (UNAVEM) will be dispatched to Angola to monitor Cuban troop withdrawal very soon. Our agent inside the UN, was a Spanish Military Officer, sadly, no longer in place. We do not have time to find and recruit a new agent. You match the profile very well. We believe we can put you in place to take up his position. We, I, can deal with the UN side to put you in position"

I raised my eyebrows and spoke again, "It's a ridiculous ask. How can I replace a Spanish Officer? People will surely know him by sight. I assume I will have to speak Spanish, that's impossible for such a long period." It was usual in these situations to remain in character for a few hours at the very most, I would need to be in place for who knows how long, weeks, months?

Roger went on undeterred, "No, we believe we can put you in place at the first UN briefing. We, the UK, is not a supplier of military personnel for the UNAVEM. Contributors will be, Algeria, Argentina, Brazil, Congo, Czechoslovakia, India, Jordan, Norway, Spain and Yugoslavia. On 1st January 1989, an advance party of 18 military observers will arrive in the capital city Luanda. Out of those 18, we believe none have ever met or have known this particular Officer before. We need a presence in Angola, as there are interested parties, including us the Brits, that feel Russian involvement, through the Cuban forces present, will try to destabilise the peace plans. You may know Angola is mineral-rich, we are certain Russia would prefer to prevent the West, with China, from benefiting from those minerals. Angola is the second-largest oil-producing country in sub-Saharan Africa with an output of approximately 1.55 million barrels of oil per day and an estimated 17,904.5 million cubic feet of natural gas production. The country has huge natural resources such as phosphates, iron ore, diamonds, bauxite, uranium, feldspar and petroleum. Exporting 40% to China, followed by the United States, India, France, Taiwan, South Africa and Canada. Through Cuba, Russia, we believe, would love to have control of these resources. The Russians are not official protagonists in this war. The Soviet Union and Cuba became especially sympathetic towards the MPLA and supplied that party with arms, ammunition, funding, and training. They also backed UNITA militants until it became clear that the latter was at irreconcilable odds with the MPLA. We want you to report to us any information you can discover regarding Russian military hardware, and if you can observe Russian personnel taking any active role in Angola. Of course, you will need to do this while acting as a UN observer, one of the 18, it won't be easy."

I had a few questions but thought better of asking right now, I would get answers to most of them later. The one question I had right now was "What happened to our agent?"

'C' replied, "All I can say right now is he has been compromised."

"So how can I replace him, he could walk in at the same time as I do?" I was getting worried, this seemed so hit and miss.

"We know that he has been terminally compromised, I will talk to you in-depth later when I have more, leave it at that Andy" I knew 'C' and trusted him, I could tell there was more to this and he wasn't saying. I found it interesting how he avoided at any time using the word "killed". Maybe this was an effort to avoid me having any concerns about the danger I would be in by replacing the Spanish agent.

I thought for about two seconds looking at 'C'. He was staring back at me waiting for me to speak. "It seems to me, I don't have much choice. It seems to me, this is a really half-baked plan. It seems to me, this job could be quite interesting. Therefore, I agree with one condition, that is, there will be in place an emergency extraction plan for me if I am compromised. I think I do not need to be in Angola longer than necessary. It's a huge area to cover, almost impossible I'd say, and it's a long long time to stay in character."

'C' spoke again, "Andy, I appreciate your answer. We will have a plan to extract you, Roger will take that on board himself", he turned to Roger, "That should be simple enough, yes?" Roger nodded in the affirmative. "The time you have to prepare yourself is very tight indeed. It will not be a simple situation at all. I'm not going to put you into the theatre of operation unless I see you are completely confident that you can remain in character, which goes without saying. Not only is the ground difficult, but the war is also brutal and dirty. I want you ready and in position January 1 that is the start date of the UNAVEM. That is three weeks. A tough call by any means. We will meet here again - let's say, December 27". He said, confirming with his assistant Max. Roger looked uncomfortable with that, I assume because of the extremely short time in which to prepare for the mission. Roger added, "There is a briefing meeting in Geneva before that date, Andy realistically needs to be ready a week earlier."

'C' asked me "Can you do this Andy?"

"If all the paperwork etc. is ready, I will" I replied a little overconfidently.

"Jean this is to be your full-time engagement it's 24/7, get Andy ready." Then 'C' spoke to us all, "If any of you are unsure, the slightest sign Andy is not ready, report to me your concerns, and I will call it off". Everyone acknowledged Chris in the affirmative. We all agreed and confirmed the appointment date. 'C' left the room with Max, with no further word. Roger handed me the file, it was marked 'SECRET' the fourth highest classification out of the five security levels the British Intelligence use. On opening the folder, each document was marked 'UK EYES ONLY'. This was a high-level operation. Personally, I felt honoured I should be asked, that I should be singled out as capable. The reality was, I was shitting myself. It would be such a huge task just to get to where I could live, breath and appear to be another person, but add to that, Angola was such a dangerous place to be, hot, wild animals, a war, and what I didn't know at the time, Angola is one of the most heavily mined countries in the world, with over 91 million square metres of land contaminated and over 1,200 known minefields. Millions of landmines and other unexploded bombs are scattered throughout the country -the legacy of over 40 years of the conflict. This wasn't going to be easy at all. Why did I want to do it? It was my job and that is what I'm paid to do. Could I refuse the request? This wasn't an order, 'C' never once inferred it was, but I suspected my career would have taken a sabbatical if I turned it down, the service needs brave people. One thing for sure, this was going to be my toughest assignment yet.

Roger read through each document aloud so that we could discuss any matter that arose. I felt there was something about him I didn't like, I couldn't put my finger on what it was about him - yet.

It would be easy to leave the situation if needed by simply faking an illness, that part was easy. The linguist Jean asked me to talk to her only in Spanish, I would need to spend a lot of time perfecting the language and accent to sound as native as possible, but fortunately, the person I was about to impersonate had a British mother, so a slight British twang to my voice could be excused. The language of Angola was Portuguese, I didn't know a single word of it, that wasn't important, and chances are few of the other UN staff present would know the language either. I asked Roger how he was sure no other person in the UN delegation would know I wasn't who I would say I was. He confirmed, as there were only 18 observers in the initial phase, as Spain was such a large country he was sure no other Spanish UN observer would realise I was an impersonator if I could keep in character. My new persona would be Comandante Anselmo Gil. I questioned the name, it was way too similar to my own. Documents were being produced, passport, passes, driving licence, bank accounts, a military record, school history, birth certificate, everything. According to Roger, the surname Gil is the 24th ranking surname in Spain, with 72 thousand people having the name, it was common. At least I could sign my initials without thinking. There was no time to lose, I would start work and become a new identity immediately. It wasn't going to be easy, while at home I would be English, at work Spanish.

17. Comandante Anselmo Gil

I spent some hours at the Reform Club that day, I began to learn who my character was. Jean was very patient with me, I always struggled with languages, and it wasn't a natural thing for me. However, I could speak conversational Spanish, I'd learnt the language during training, and had holidayed in Spain many times and I hoped one day to buy a property for holidays, it is my favourite country. Roger informed me as much as he knew about Comandante Anselmo Gil.

We worked until there was a danger I might miss the last train home. I'd have to get a train back to Amersham on the Metropolitan Line, where, I'd pick up the company van and drive the last part of the journey in order to appear to my wife Julie that I'd spent a late night at the printers again.

Every day for the next 3 weeks was spent with Jean, though in different surroundings. We rented a conference room at a beautiful hotel, the De Vere Latimer Estate, in Chesham. Certainly, a lovely place to work. It enabled me to spend more time learning, rather than spend time each day travelling back and forth, as it was only 25 minutes' drive from my home in Aylesbury.

We worked hard to perfect my Spanish language. I'd learn everything about Anselmo by listening and speaking only Spanish to make it as natural as possible, it also helped to learn technical words used in the Spanish army too. My uniform arrived with the insignia for the rank of Comandante, along with all my papers. I also received a set of civilian clothes all with Spanish labels. My personal effects were all Spanish, there wasn't to be a single clue that I wasn't Spanish at all. I would get my UN uniform when I attended a briefing meeting for all nationalities in the 18 man delegation at United Nations, Geneva in mid-December.

By the last week of December, learning my cover was complete, I had been tested thoroughly, people would call my English name to try to trick me, to see if I reacted in the smallest way. Sometimes I would be holding a conversation in Spanish, Jean or whoever was talking to me would throw in a line in English to see if I noticed. I knew Anselmo's personal and military background as perfectly as was possible. To get to the UN meeting in Geneva, Switzerland, I had to fly first to Barcelona, Spain, on a diplomatic flight, the British Consulate General in Barcelona represents the UK government in Catalonia. Then drive to Madrid, so that staff at Madrid Airport would not recognise me and possibly notice I had arrived from London. Then, onward via a Swissair flight to Geneva, tickets provided by the UN. I arrived in character of course, although, I kept to myself as much as possible, I was more comfortable that way. At the briefing we were given our assigned locations, pre-deployment Training Materials (CPTMs) and a full mandate of rules and regulations, ending the day with a test in order to confirm each of us understood the UN regulations and everything that went with it. Everything handed to me at the UN was in English, even though by now I was fully competent in the Spanish language, I had no problem with that side of things. Military observer teams were to verify and record all movements of Cuban military personnel and equipment in and out of Angola. The ports of Cabinda, Lobito, Luanda and Namibe, and also Luanda airport were the five main centres where the UN would be based, Luanda being the Headquarters. But there were mobile teams that were to observe and confirm Cuban redeployment, northward from locations south of the 13th parallel. This was the team I was assigned, thanks to Roger's insider circle of influence. Each foreign observer had local assistants made up of police and officials. All in all, there were 50,000 Cuban troops withdrawing from Angola. The entire UN mission was led by Chief Military Observer Brigadier-General Péricles Ferreira Gomes of Brazil, who seemed quite a congenial as well as a professional man. After the Geneva meeting, I returned home by reversing the route I had taken to get there.

I would have to come up with a plan to cover me being away from home. I should have told the truth to Julie, I didn't, that was a huge mistake and I have regretted that ever since. Maybe because I had so much else on my mind, maybe stress, maybe given the amount I was having to take on, whatever the reason, home life took a step back. Instead, I chose to devise a story to cover my time away. I'd be going sailing, I'd be going on a cruise. Julie didn't like sailing at all, she never wanted to come with me, that's what made that lie so easy. In all honesty not being honest about my second life was always a big, big mistake. It would have been easy to tell her the truth. She had already been security checked, there was no reason at all not to be honest. I should have told her what I did from the start, but because what happened with Janine and the fact I never thought we'd stay together, the moment always seemed to pass until it was too late. I regret it to this day. How could I suddenly tell her I wasn't who she thought I was, how could I tell her I'd been lying to her all these years. I wish I could justify how I treated Julie, and Janine too, but realistically I can't. It had reached the point where it was too late to tell her.

A plan was put in place for me to go on a sailing cruise, Sailing Schools ran courses and cruises all year round, I had actually been on one in December a year before, it was cold but the air was clear and the night sky was always amazing at that time of year. The school's yachts have heaters, it wasn't unpleasant, and there is something about being in the cold all day then sitting somewhere warm and cosy at night, that helped me sleep well. If I needed to stay longer in Angola, a plan was in position for me to pretend to have an accident, I'd be hit on the head by a swinging boom, a common enough accident on a yacht, they are heavy things. I had prepared photographs of me in a hospital bed with a concussion, in order to send them to her if the need arose. It was not a serious enough accident to warrant her travelling over to join me. It would be a reason to delay my return home. The UNAVEM was expected to run for at least six months, I would never stay that long. To my mind, the whole plan was very shoddy. It wasn't my plan it was Roger's, I was never happy with it, but I just got on with it as that is what was asked of me. I don't blame 'C' for allowing such a dreadful plan to proceed, I could see he wasn't happy with it either. Maybe that is why Roger had a desk job, he just wasn't that smart. My guess was that probably the 'old boy' network had got him his job, he was of that upper-class type, and I didn't like him. There was always something about Roger that I didn't find right, call it my sixth sense.

I was happy I had my character perfect, Jean was happy with my linguistics, my accent was good, I could get away with a very slight Englishness to my speech because Anselmo had an English mother. I had got through the meeting for the UN delegation in Geneva, I had my role in Angola sorted. What could possibly go wrong?

18. Moving To Angola

December 27, I was as prepared as I would ever be for my mission, half-baked as it was. I travelled to London for a final meeting with 'C' at the Reform Club before travelling on to the UN. At the meeting was me, 'C', Max, Roger. There was no need for Jean to be present, her job was complete and she had already given me a pass as far as my language ability was concerned. 'C' opened the meeting. He asked me if I thought I was ready and if I was happy with all the arrangements. By now my attitude toward Roger was that he was an upper-class twat. His plan was so bad and I was going along with it. I told 'C' as much. He asked me if I thought the mission should be aborted. It probably should have been, but I said that everything I needed was in place, I'd passed all tests, including Geneva, and I saw no real reason to call it off at this stage. In hindsight, I shouldn't have gone along with Roger's plan at all. I should have asked for a better planner, but at the end of the day it was my shout and I was the one to blame if it all went wrong. Roger had worked hard getting the paperwork sorted, somehow he had got everything at the UN in place. I handed 'C' a file that I had written, containing a mission statement, something not always done in situations like this, but I had decided in this case it was a good move.

The mission statement explained the method I would use to hopefully find Russians in such a short time. The back plan was if there was a mole in MI6, I was hoping I would be exposed and compromised by the traitor, thus revealing not only the presence of Russians in a country they were not supposed to be operating militarily but also potentially expose the mole that I was now convinced existed within MI6. It was the real reason I personally thought the mission should continue, in my mind the presence of Russians in Angola was secondary. If I don't mind saying, it was a bloody dangerous strategy, and I was the bait. I wrote the mission statement and it was down to me. I'd be in contact with SIS daily by using a secret coded data burst transmitter. At the end of the meeting, 'C' took me aside alone. "Andy, you realise what you are doing, and the danger you will constantly be in. Are you really sure this one will work?"

"Can only try" was my blunt reply.

He asked me what I thought of Roger, I didn't understand the question. I told 'C' what I thought of Roger and I'd be glad when I don't have to see him again. He reassured me that in the event I needed to get out I could send a distress message, and urgent rescue would be forthcoming. The mission was given a go.

I had packed my bags, Roger checked through everything to make sure there wasn't one single item that would give away the fact I wasn't Spanish. One item or set of items he pulled out was that I had several football shirts. In my experience, if ever one needed to make friends somewhere, give them a Manchester United football shirt, it was international currency and never failed wherever one was in the world to make a friend for life. I had an entire team of shirts. After a short discussion, it was decided I could take the shirts. I was taken by car to Gatwick airport for my flight to Barcelona.

In Barcelona again, I drove to Madrid. From there, I'd fly to Geneva where all the delegates would be gathering. We travelled on a white United Nations Boeing 737 aeroplane to Luanda, Angola's capital city. On the flight, the delegates got to know each other a little and was uneventful. Arriving at Luanda, on the apron of the airfield we disembarked and gathered to listen to a speech by a local dignitary. He welcomed us and wished us well and a successful mission. The speech went on for 10 minutes it seemed so much more. It was hot standing there, tired after our journey and we needed to get somewhere more comfortably cool. I don't know why they thought it a good idea to hold us in the heat. By the time the speech was finished my shirt was soaked with sweat. We collected our bags ourselves, there didn't seem to be any baggage handlers at all. Cars arrived to take us to the UN village that had been prepared for us just south of the airport.

A UN village of white tents had been erected, an entire infrastructure had been created. We were billeted in white Weatherhaven tents, a tube shape tent with windows and a wooden door on one end. Inside was a hardwood floor, electric lights and nice reasonably comfortable cots, two people per tent, and an air-conditioning unit, without which we would have certainly roasted. There were food tents, a hospital tent, which was already occupied with patients, which surprised me. Toilet tents and showers completed our basic needs. The complete infrastructure was well planned and almost self-sufficient. It was a bit like glamping in a war zone but with hot weather. We had a few hours to settle in, get food and showered, which I desperately needed by now. I was living and breathing Spanish, nobody appeared to suspect I wasn't who I claimed to be, probably because everyone was too excited or nervous to be in a war zone to pay close attention to me.

There was a range of vehicles, Landcruisers, Jeeps and cars of various makes. Most of us would need to move on to our respective areas of operation at the four ports where Cuban troops and equipment were due to embark. Those monitoring Luanda airport, of course, would remain at this camp. I was to head of one of the mobile units, our life in Angola would be much more uncomfortable. We would have to move out quite quickly to other locations to the east of the country to monitor the northward movement of Cuban units to positions above the 13th parallel. The UNAVEM was due to begin on January 1st, there was only a couple of days in which we all had to get into position. My particular area was way over on the east side of the country in the province of Moxico. Quite possibly the most inhospitable area, it is said it was the most mined area in the world. We would have to be very cautious and avoid moving off-road at all times. Moxico had been identified as the area most likely to have evidence of Russian military personnel and hardware. The camp that was established for my group had been prepared and ready for us to move into. We would take a small aircraft to Luena, the capital city of Moxico, where land vehicles were waiting for us. As I was group leader, I could order the camp to move to wherever I needed, when I received information Cuban troops would be moving and that the roads were clear of mines. The UK intelligence had given me satellite photos of the area, I had coordinates of places of interest. I was most interested in the areas around Samucheque, Lumbala, Nhamuana, and Cacande where there were some hidden airstrips quite suitable for secret army camps to be set up by Cubans or Russians. I had been briefed by Roger that Russian personnel may well be situated in Moxico. It wouldn't be a problem, as I was in charge, to order my team of UN observers to take a drive to wherever I wanted to go, provided it was safe, the war was still going on, despite the withdrawal of the Cubans, which was the first phase to the supposed end to the hostilities.

19. Moxico, Not A Holiday Destination

My team and I flew to Luena airport about 500 miles south-east of Luanda, a smaller airport than Luanda, where our camp was already prepared by the advanced teams. The flight was not without its tension, as we knew surface to air missiles were deployed in-country, with a range of 39,000 feet we were definitely sitting targets. It's not a comfortable feeling sitting in an aeroplane with no defence system and a war going on 7 miles below.

The town of Luena seemed normal, there were obvious signs of war of course, but people were going about their daily business. Our camp was on some ground to the south and west of the airport, about five minutes' drive. There were signs of war here, men were openly carrying weapons in the streets. The language spoken here was chokwe, but some Portuguese was evident on signs around town. January wasn't the best time to be in Moxico province, the rainy season would soon start and travel by road could become impossible, especially as many dirt roads, (there were few good tarmac roads) were war damaged too. The locals were often quick to repair them, as they needed the roads for trade, I was sure that the military would prefer easy road access too. This gave me a real sense that I should not hang around, I needed to get to the more remote places as soon as possible, I didn't want to get stuck somewhere far out in the field because the road had washed away. Praying on my mind too was my sailing cover story was good for only two weeks.

In three cars, with a trusted local official as a guide, we set about visiting the Cuban military bases in Luena without delay. Clearly, the Cubans were packed and ready to move north and then west, as they had agreed to do according to the UN Security Council resolution. They were friendly enough toward our group. The Cuban Commander showed me maps of planned military movements under his command. We spoke in Spanish, but Cuban characteristics made the language a little difficult for me to understand at first. I planned to leave one car in Luena, with its crew of one UN observer and three locals to observe the Cuban troop movements due to start the next day, after which we would regroup when we returned from our trip further east. I could see little evidence of Russian personnel, although it would have been easy for them to stay out of sight.

Before leaving England I had been given satellite imagery of a few locations of interest to SIS at home in London. I had studied these, and knew I'd need to get close to those areas soon before the rains, and, because I wanted to spend as little time as possible in Angola. One such area was around the small town of Lumbala on the Zambezi River about 25 miles north of the border with Zambia on the 13th parallel. Unusually, the border in that area is a perfectly straight line from east to west, then takes a 90-degree turn north to south, again in a dead straight line. I decided to set off with the group early the next day. There is a road that heads south from Luena which gradually sweeps easterly toward Lumbala. At 5 am just as first light was starting to appear on the horizon, we set off in our two Landcruisers packed with tents, food, water and fuel in order to make camp at our destination. We would wear civilian clothing, we felt it safer to avoid confusion given the number of different forces involved in the conflict. We felt a soldier seeing a uniform not recognised as his own may treat us as hostile. We did, however, continue to wear the light blue beret of the UN and the vehicles had UN flags flying. The camp at Luena would remain as a base for our return to in a few days. The locals had told us that the road was good but in places very difficult. Some sections of the road may be impassable in the rain. It was a major trade road but by our standards narrow and a rough dirt road, it passed through many villages where there was small scale digging for minerals, the local people kept the road open as much and for as long as possible when it became rain damaged. It would be a long drive, about 240 miles, even if we could maintain 30 miles per hour it would be an 8-hour drive. With 12.5 hours sunlight in January, taking into account driving breaks, refuelling, slow sections and anything else, including conflict, we were going to be hard pushed to make Lumbala in a day, but local advice claimed it was possible to complete the journey before dark.

Note: There is more than one Lumbala in Angola. The Lumbala discussed here is at 12°38'30"S 22°35'18"E.

After last-minute checks that we had everything we needed for the journey, we set out of the UN camp, and very soon we were heading into the countryside on the EN180 main route to Lumbala. The road was better than expected and we made very good progress. We stopped a few times to have a break and say hello to the locals to try to get information on the route ahead. There was always the possibility of running into a military skirmish, roadblocks or mines, it was always good to receive local knowledge on the road ahead. We were aware these stops would add time to our journey but we felt it better to have fore-knowledge of the roads ahead. Comfort breaks were always in a township on the road, we felt it wise not to wander behind some bushes because of the risk of mines. As we drove along the road, we saw many red signs warning of mines. At Lucusse about 4 hours into our journey, we made a stop for refreshments. Here was the first sign of the danger that these people lived every day. There was a school and next to the school on a fence, were red mine warning signs. In the field next to the school, cattle were grazing seemingly unaware of the danger they must be in, luckily we didn't witness any cows being blown up. At the boundary as we entered the town there was an airfield, basically, a dirt track cleared for a runway. People told us that Cuban troops had been stationed there, but had now left. We marked this on our UN map and noted the information people gave us what military company it was.

Lucusse seemed as good a place as any to eat. We stood around our vehicles stretching our legs and talking to any locals that came to take a look at us. Our light blue berets, of course, were a bit of a novelty, but most people had heard that the UN was trying hard to bring an end to so many years of war and the killing and destruction that brings. It was impossible to mark all of the minefields, there were simply just too many of them. It was obvious that it was going to take years if ever at all, to make this land safe again. The locals, however, did seem to be going about daily business quite normally and shops were stocked, even if a little meagrely.

Back in our vehicles again, it was nice to feel the benefit of the air-conditioning, for me the heat was my biggest enemy. Making the mistake to not drink enough water, thinking it would avoid the need to stop for comfort breaks too often. My head started to spin and I was sweating gallons, it didn't take long to learn, no matter how much water I drunk, I would sweat it out rather than need to pee. Passing through the town, we had to take a left turn onto another road that led to Lumbala, we thought it would be about three more hours' drive. But now the road narrowed and became less easy to keep up our speed. We passed through another village that we didn't stop at, as time was beginning to worry us more. The village was literally about 400 yards long and one street wide, shortly after this we reached a lake. The road bridge crossed the water at a place where the lake narrowed but the bridge had been destroyed. We headed back to the village where local people informed us we should double back the way we came, about a mile, where we should take a sharp turn to the north and circumvent the lake on a narrower dustier road. We knew if it started to rain now we would not be able to return this way, but we could not let that stop us, we would have to worry about that if it happened. The detour probably added about 5 miles to our journey.

Once we re-joined the original road, we started to see more evidence of small scale mining for minerals, there were small ponds of bright green or blue water. A further eight miles, and the first of several bridges that had definitely seen better days appeared in front of us. It appeared to be made of wood with the top planks quite loose. I walked ahead of the vehicles to take a look to make sure it was safe. While I was looking and jumping on some of the planks in a vain hope of being able to tell if they would hold, a couple of locals walked up to me and happily reassured me it was safe. I reported this to our drivers. All passengers got out of the cars and we let the drivers' inch across alone in the vehicles. It wasn't a long or particularly high bridge about twenty-five feet across and about ten feet high, but enough that no one fancied being in the vehicles as they crossed. The bridge held well with a few of the planks rattling a little, quite uneventful really, but I was glad to be out of the car rather than stay in it. On the other side of the dry river bed was a steep climb up a hill, again letting us know in the rain this would become a very different journey.

There followed a stretch of road, that, in another country would be quite amazing to witness. Every 200 yards on the north side of the road were diggings, each one about 25 yards wide and 100 yards long. Perhaps each one was a dug by a family, we didn't stop to ask. But this went on for about 18 miles, dig after dig, most of them dry, some filled with bluish-green water. At least now this section of road was a less hilly dirt road. Eventually, we reached a village called Kinjama. With about 50 houses running parallel to the road. It was time for another leg stretch, so we took a break and made small talk with the villagers who gathered to see the blue berets. Everyone we met seemed to know and to expect to see UN observers, we found no hostility toward us at all. Everyone seemed friendly enough. There were still some red mine warning signs along the road, I'm not sure how the people here dug for the minerals without blowing themselves up. Maybe they did, there were certainly a few people with lost limbs, but who knows if their injuries were from mines or war. I gave out a few sweets or bandages if it looked as though they could benefit from a clean one.

After a short break, we took to the road yet again. Almost immediately coming across yet another poorly built wooden bridge, only this one was obviously unsafe to drive across. We could easily take a left where it was clear from tracks in the dirt, that people before us had taken a small detour around the bridge.

Fig. 3 Unusable bridge, we dropped down into the dry riverbed, but if it rained this would become unpassable.

The track dipped down and took a horseshoe turn over the almost dry river bed, yet again letting us know if the rain came there would not be a way back on this road. After the climb up from the river crossing, there was mile after mile of digging pits on either side of the road. From space or a plane, this road must have looked like a long zipper. It carried on like this for at least 80 miles. There was the odd truck on the road but, we didn't see much in the way of the military, which was a little odd, but maybe they just didn't fight on the road. The few military vehicles we did see were only trucks with groups of armed men, no heavy artillery or tanks, only lightly armed troops. They never bothered us, save for shouting and waving at us, the blue flags on our vehicles were clearly working. We hoped nobody wanted to create an international incident by making trouble, although we did feel a little intimidated by these men, they could easily have robbed us.

Eventually, the bushland we had experienced for so many miles turned into woods. Wc could still see in the trees people digging their mineral pits, mile after mile we drove through the trees, we had been driving, with stops for ten hours. Finally, the road dropped down a bank and the Zambezi River came into view. We could see part of Lumbala village on our side of the river, but the main village was on the east side. We easily found the platform ferry to cross to the other side and drove up the river bank on a sloped road that joined the EN190 north into the village. We had taken ten hours to drive to Lumbala and had about 2 hours light to make camp somewhere suitable and reasonably safe. Almost the entire village came out to meet us when we pulled up, we were led to the village elder or mayor, Filipe Lolo Lomba, a tall thin man who greeted us kindly, and, after introductions, led us to his house which surprisingly had a large garden completely surrounded by a wall. He said we could make our camp inside the walled garden, which must have stretched for 100 yards by 100 yards. Clearly, he was a man of wealth, and we got on very well with him. In return for his hospitality in a hastily arranged ceremony, I presented him and the village with an entire set of Manchester United football shirts. The villagers seemed more than happy, they clapped and spontaneously started to dance. I guessed we were going to be safe here for the duration of our stay.

We set up our camp, not an easy task with villagers wanting to help, they just got in the way. But we eventually got them to leave with Mr Lomba chivvying them away to leave us and his garden in peace. Inside the walls of his garden, there was an inner walled garden surrounding his house in a rectangle. We camped inside this space in the shade of some fruit trees, effectively we had two walls protecting us from the outside. We were very tired after our long journey. We cooked up some food on our stoves, boosted by fruit and fresh vegetables brought to us by Mr Lomba's wife. It would have been more diplomatic to eat and talk with Mr Lomba that evening, but quite frankly we were all exhausted. We said we would talk in more depth tomorrow, he understood and left us to rest and sleep.

20. Mr Filipe Lomba

The next morning, I woke at 5 am, it was still dark, and there would be another hour before the dawn would cast any light on our surroundings. In our tents the group was still sleeping, I could hear a roaring snore in one tent. How the poor person sleeping in the tent with him got any sleep I will never know. I quietly left my tent and stood in the fresh air and stretched. This could be such a lovely country if only these people could stop fighting each other. There were enough minerals in this wild country to make everyone rich, but I guess that's why they fight, for power and wealth. I shaved and found a tree to hang a shower bag and washed wearing only my underwear, it was nice to feel clean again after the long and dusty journey yesterday. I dressed after covering myself with mosquito repellent. I am one of those people that mosquitoes love to eat, I can be covered in bites while everyone else remains untouched by them, I have no idea why. We were very lucky this village seemed so friendly. I put a pot of water on the gas burner to make some coffee. By the time I had finished my ablutions, I saw a light come on in Mr Lomba's house. I wondered how he had made himself so obviously prosperous. While waiting for my coffee pot to heat up I walked silently around his garden. It was the only garden I had seen since arriving in Angola that was landscaped and tidy. Cut grass, flowers and fruit trees made his garden an oasis from the squalor outside these walls.

Mr Lomba appeared in his doorway, so I went over to say hello and have a chat. He invited me into his house for coffee. I quickly turned off the gas under my water pot as he ushered me inside. By western standards, his home was simply furnished, but in this country, it was very comfortable.

I thanked him again, "Thank you, Sir, for your most kind hospitality, you have such a wonderful home and your villagers clearly love you."

Now, normally I never call anyone Sir, it's a thing of mine. In my opinion, Sir is a mark of respect. Bullies such as teachers, can say and call you anything they like, but you have no recourse to answer back in the same manner, they do not deserve to be called 'Sir'. I went through all my school days and never once called any teacher 'Sir' or 'Miss'. Except for Miss Willox, firstly because she was unmarried so it was her correct title, but secondly because despite being the strictest teacher I had for the entirety of my education, was fair and human. I never gave any of my bosses at work the title Sir, because, well, because I just don't, they probably earned the title, according to my own rules, but I just never did.

Mr Lomba, however, was different. I immediately could see he was an oasis of peace and sensibility, he had made a comfortable home for himself and his wife in a country that had been ripped by war for decades, he was liked by the people in this town. He deserved respect, and at the end of the day I now represent the United Nations, I should afford him the honour accordingly. I liked this man.

We spoke in English, with me faking a Spanish accent, as this was the common language between us. "Welcome into my home Comandante, let me get you some coffee when your team is awake my wife will make you all some nice breakfast, bread and eggs" he started "I hope you are staying today, later she will make you Calulu. I want to say, Anselmo, your gift of those football shirts was such a fine gesture to my people, you have made the kids so happy. We have now George Best and Bobby Charlton in our village ha-ha. It is the best gift you give us."

"You are very welcome Filipe, I hope it brings pleasure to the kids. Please call me Anselmo, we have no need for formalities." I asked, "What is Calulu?"

"Then you must call me Filipe please and please sit at my table. Calulu is a local dish of fish stew, we will make you our special guests here"

"You have a lovely home Filipe, how did you create such a garden, it is beautiful"

While we sat opposite each other in his kitchen at a small table drinking coffee, he explained he owned all the village. He had ventured here 10 years ago, the war had begun and was clear it was getting very dirty. His family had been slaughtered and he escaped from Chemboca a small town to the south and west from here. About 100 miles as the crow flies, I guessed he must have travelled three times that by road at least to get here.

I admired him even more for his bravery and tenacity.

"How did you make your fortune?" it was clear he had become rich here, it wasn't a forward question.

"When I came here there was nothing, but I camped here one night as I was travelling, I was aiming for Cazombo to the north where I have some relatives. I found by accident a diamond, just lying there next to me in the morning when I woke. I thought to myself, this is a sign, I must stay here and dig. You saw the diggings on the road on the other side of the river. Many are my digs. I found diamonds, so many, so I employed people to come and help me dig and this village grew from nothing."

"That's incredibly lucky from such a bad beginning Filipe. How do you stop the people you employ from stealing from you?"

"At first it was some family that came to help me, then as things got busier and the digs became more productive, I have employed trusted people. I pay them well, but you see, they can't sell the diamonds, they would have to leave the village to sell them and I would know."

We chatted small talk for a few minutes, I liked this man more after hearing his story, such a brave and strong man, yet his manner is so calm and peaceful.

I changed the subject. "Filipe, there is an airfield just up the road, I see it on photographs I have been given. Are there any MPLA or Cubans here? We need to monitor their withdrawal, it's why we came here."

"Anselmo, you need to be careful, there is a military camp the other side of the airstrip it is MPLA and Cubans. We try to avoid them. The Cubans, with Russian help, want to make this place Communist. They will steal everything I have here. I pay them in diamonds to let me continue my business, and we supply them food. Not because we care for them, but to save our lives. They will slaughter us if we stop. I am waiting for this moment the UN arrive, and now I can watch them leave."

"The problem I have Filipe is that the camp you say is there is not on any map the UN has given me. So I need to approach them, I have a feeling the camp will be one that Cuba will try to keep secret, essentially to break the peace that has been negotiated. They know the wealth here is great and you know they won't let it out of their hands easily. I will need to contact the UN headquarters about this."

This was the reason I was here for both UN and UK intelligence. I had to get closer to try to see if the Russians were here with military personnel and weapons if they were hiding from the world this would be significant. The UK would use any information I can glean.

"Filipe, have you seen any military hardware at the camp?"

"The airstrip is too short for large carrier planes, we built it so that diamond buyers in light planes can come and do business. But I have seen and hear sometimes military aircraft, very loud because they rev the engines to stop on the short runway and make such a noise. I am sure some weapons have arrived here. But we avoid contact, we don't want communism and the MPLA are brutal people. We just want to live in peace and go about our business. I am living in fear of being killed for my business, but I think they are lazy, they prefer us to do the hard work while they drink beer and sit with their feet up."

I needed to see the camp, it would be very dangerous for sure. I couldn't put my UN team in such danger, normally I think we should have reported the situation to the UN and left the area quickly before we are discovered here. But my alter-mission was to investigate and report to SIS. I would have to do this alone, without the UN team, if they knew the situation here they would want to leave immediately, it was far too dangerous.

I was about to make the worst decision in my life.

21. This Is Not Good.

I finished my coffee with Filipe and told him I should go check on my team and tell them to rise for breakfast and to make plans to backtrack a few miles for safety. There we could take stock of the situation and await instructions from the UN.

I thanked Filipe Lomba for the coffee and chat and left the house, promising to return shortly for breakfast with the team. Outside the sun was now on the horizon. The remaining seven members of my team were getting dressed and ready for the day. One car was still in Luena observing movements there, and acting as our base camp group. I informed the team of the situation in a group meeting. Most of the team wanted to leave right away. I said they should have breakfast in the house first, then we'd make a move to withdraw a few miles west across the river again, that at least would give us some protection. A couple of the team were a little shaken by the realisation of the danger we were now in, I reassured them our cars were inside the compound, so were we, this afforded us some protection by being out of sight from the village. The main road was 300 yards from Filipe's house, I judged we were not in immediate danger at that moment. But, it would be wise to have breakfast, break camp and leave ASAP.

Filipe arrived to lead us into his house, the team followed him and disappeared into the kitchen for a nice breakfast. I stayed outside for a few moments to pack my stuff, I'd had coffee, and I said I'd be there once I was packed. I quickly shoved my sleeping bag into its cover and put my things away. The tent would be packed away once breakfast was done.

While I was alone, I thought I'd go take a look at the MPLA camp, I hoped they'd still be asleep or at least still quite dozy as it was only 06.30 hours. With the UN team inside starting their eggs and bread, I grabbed my camera and disappeared quietly out of the front gate into the street and headed north to the airstrip no more than 200 yards away.

The airstrip had no fences around it, none did in this kind of country, it was just a clearing in the scrub and a dirt runway. I estimated the length of the runway was about 5000 feet. A Russian Antonov transport aircraft could land and take off in 4000 feet easily. The main EN190 road crosses the runway halfway along its length. I walked slowly and cautiously along the edge of the airfield toward the road, there was almost no cover at all should I need it, I did not want any of the MPLA to spot me, in retrospect, I was being quite foolish, yet, at the time I felt I needed to do what a spy should do. There was nobody around this early in the morning. There was a wooded area at the far eastern end of the landing strip. I moved quickly along to the woods to try to get some cover. On the opposite side of the runway, I could see there was a military camp. The buildings were brick or mud-built, using the cover of the few trees between me and the camp I crouched in the shadow of a tree and took a couple of photos. There were a couple of vehicles in sight, and so far I could see only civilian types such as Toyota pickup trucks. As the angle changed as I walked a little further, some military hardware did come into view. I could not identify what they were, but clearly field guns of sorts maybe a rocket system too. There wasn't any sign of anyone on guard duty, which seemed odd to me.

Further to the west, I could see smoke from a small fire, maybe there would be another camp there. To the north were more trees, but to get to them I'd need to cross the road in front of the camp, that was too dangerous I'd be too close to them. I swept back to the west to take advantage of a slope where the land begins to drop toward the river as there was still little cover from trees on this side of the road. The land was crisscrossed with paths, I guessed it was reasonably safe from mines but still my senses were the highest they could be, it's amazing how the danger of being blown up does that! Now I turned and continued east. There were a few houses to my south here, but there was no sign of anyone up yet. I crept past them as quietly as I could. I crossed the EN190 road to the east side, now I had some cover from the trees. I could see the camp clearly, it was fenced, there were some vehicles I didn't recognise I guessed they may be Russian or Cuban, they just looked that type of vehicle and definitely more military hardware of various kinds. There was a watchtower and I could see two uniformed soldiers in the shelter on top of the tower. I couldn't make out the uniform of the soldiers as they were in the shadow, it was hard to see in the early morning low light but the uniform looked darkish green.

Fig. 4 The watchtower, two guards seemed unaware I was there. The photograph was taken from the cover of trees

The guards were walking around the tower showing no sign that they had spotted me. I used the trees as cover and moved north to try to get a view of the camp from another angle. After about 200 yards there were a couple of houses, I moved around the furthest house into the clear but protected from view by the building. I took a few more photos, the camp was definitely Cuban or Russian. It was too tidy to be NPLA. As I held my camera to take pictures, the door of the house just a few feet to my left suddenly opened. Expecting to see a local I was surprised to see a white man, in uniformed trousers and shirt. Shit! I ducked behind the building and leaned back against the wall in the hope he hadn't seen me. The camp was across the road, I couldn't figure out why he was using this house outside the camp. The man suddenly appeared at the corner of the house about 3 feet from where I was leaning back against the wall in a vain attempt to keep out of sight. Behind him were two other men pointing weapons at me. As a member of the UNAVEM, I should not be acting in this way. I should not be sneaking around in the early dawn on my own. I knew I'd messed up.

"Shit, this is not good" I muttered under my breath.

22. Taken Prisoner

The two men in front of me stood for probably a quarter of a second, it seemed like thirty. The other man spoke in English with a Russian accent, "Good morning Andy, nice of you to join us."

What the hell? He was using my English name, he knew who I was! I spoke in Spanish keeping to my character. "I am Comandante Anselmo Gil UN Observer to UNAVEM acting under Security Council resolution 626. I do apologise for waking you."

He rudely interrupted me, raising his voice in anger, Russians always do. "Don't mess around Andy, I know who you are and why you are here.", then more politely he added, "You must come with me now". With that the two other men moved forward relieved me of my camera and grabbed me quite violently by my arms, pushing my head down my chin on my chest, as Russians do. I was frog-marched, held securely by the two men their strong grip really hurt my arms.

"Where are we going, you are contravening Security Council resolution 626 and violating a UN official representative" The guy in charge grabbed my hair lifting my head, threw a punch smack in the middle of my face causing my nose to start bleeding.

"Why are you pretending Andy, I know who you are, you can fuck your UN story, Britain does not represent the UN here in Angola. I am not violating anything, you are a spy, you are in civilian clothes, and I know who you are" he repeated, with that he pushed my head back down and we continued into the camp on the other side of the road.

How did he know who I am? The UN, and my team, have no idea I am not Spanish Comandante Anselmo Gil. In Britain few people in the SIS know I am here, how does this guy know me?

"May I ask who you are?" I maintained my Spanish, but I was guessing it would be pointless. He didn't reply. But a punch to a kidney let me know not to speak again until invited. I decided I didn't like the idea of receiving any more punches, so I stayed quiet until I was thrown quite violently into a small cell-like room in a hut on the military camp. The door slammed shut behind me, it would have been dark, but for a little light leaking around the edge of the door and the window that had been covered by wood panels to block anyone from looking in or out of this room. After a few moments, my eyes accustomed to the darkness, I could see the room was empty.

This most definitely wasn't good, how should I play this? Shall I maintain my Spanish pretence, or admit to who I am. Training had taught me to stick to my story, play the innocent man, pretend I know nothing, pretend that I was acting for my superiors. I could try to stick to my Spanish story for as long as I could, obviously, he knew I was Andy, which also meant he most probably knew I was MI6. But for now, I'd be Comandante Anselmo Gil. I wished now, that I had experienced the interrogation back in the UK that my fellow students had endured, but because I outsmarted the guy I was following in Gosport, I missed that experience. I'd just have to remember what I was taught and stick with it. My next concern was, where was this imprisonment going to lead? I was sure they would not release me as a UN representative and apologise for the mistake. I felt sure my captors were deciding my future right now, maybe they were speaking to some higher authority taking advice on what to do with me. What kept turning over in my brain was, how the hell did he know who I was, and, how did he know I'd be right here?

One thing was for sure, I was glad I had done my ablutions earlier, or there would be a hell of a stink in this room right now.

23. Don't Try This At Home.

I don't know how long after I was dumped unceremoniously into the dark room, it seemed like days, but was probably minutes before the door was thrown open by the two men that had dragged me here. The light blinded me for a second or two. They brought into the room a small wooden table and two chairs. I was grabbed and dumped into the chair facing the door.

I tried pointless humour "Thank you gentlemen, tell me, in this part of the world do you put the jam on top or the clotted cream on top of your scone? Two sugars in my tea thank you" A huge mistake on my part as this was clearly an English reference to cream teas, but my fear was not letting me think too clearly right now. I forgave myself of the error I was sure nerves were playing a part. Clearly, the waiters here didn't expect a tip, as my attempt to lighten the situation with humour resulted with a punch to my ear, strong enough to make me fall sideways off the chair, all I could hear was a whistling noise. While on the floor the other guy gave me a nice kick to my right ribs, I felt a rib snap, leaving me with some difficulty in breathing. It felt as though every time I breathed in, the rib was pressing into my diaphragm below my lungs. I moaned as I tried to sit back up. I looked up from the ground just in time to see another boot heading toward my face. On contact it broke a molar on my right lower jaw, it hurt like crazy, but I wasn't going to give these bully boys the pleasure of seeing me scared or in pain, just as I would always deal with bullies as a kid.

"I hope your meat here isn't tough, I think I'll be having trouble chewing now". I should have stopped my attempts at humour, it was getting me into to trouble, they tried to inflict more pain on me with one of them grabbing my now very sore jaw and lifting me back into the seat. I didn't wince but I couldn't stop a tear in my eye from forming.

"OK, I said in English, I'll sit quietly, may I see the wine list?" I flinched waiting for my next blow, none came, "Ah, you like English" I said as they turned to leave the room.

I needed to use this time alone to asses my situation.

What was going to be the outcome? I could only see there would be one end to this. He has already told me he knows I am a spy, there is usually only one end to spies, at best I'll spend time in jail somewhere, at worse… I didn't want to think about it.

How do they know who I am, and how do they know I would be right here at this time? It can only be that there is another mole inside SIS, what's more, that mole is providing up to date information. My earlier suspicions are true.

Who is the mole? Not an important question to answer at this moment, knowing who the mole is right now will not affect the outcome of my incarceration. I decided not to worry about this question for now. If I discover who the mole may be, how do I get that information out of here, there is nothing I can do.

What do I admit, what do I tell? My situation here can only get worse. It will be highly unlikely that he will return into the room and say sorry it's a big mistake, accept our apologies and go home. Right now I do not know what it is that they want to know. The truth is, I know so little. If they know I am here in Angola, they probably know a lot. I can make stuff up, chances are the mole will confirm I'm lying to my interrogator and that will make matters worse for me. Training tells me I should hold off saying anything for as long as possible.

Is there a chance of rescue? Little, my government are not going to admit they have planted a spy inside the UN not only that, they are not going to admit to impersonating a Spanish Officer either. My government finds it hard to admit to spies that have been exposed, look at the Cambridge five, even once they had been found to be traitors, little happened to them.

The best thing I can do for myself is to do as we were taught and to look for a way out of this, an impossible task in this situation.

Would anyone at home realise my situation? Highly unlikely. This is such a mess, I've been so unprofessional. I've come here with such a short time to fully prepare. Yes, I've got the language and fake identity, but really, I have made the mistake of trying to achieve something that should require at least six months to do the job properly. I gave myself two weeks in Angola. I've had to make up a story to cover my absence from home. If only Julie knew beforehand, then I could have taken time to do this properly.

I need to think clearly for as long as I can, I'm sure they will wear me down in the end, I need to eat if they offer food, I need to sleep if I get a chance.

I sat at the table in the dark room my head spinning with too many questions. One thing for sure, I need to stop making a joke of everything and start taking this as seriously as the situation deserves, no one will appreciate bravado.

After sitting alone for just a couple of minutes, the door opened letting in a burst of light that forced my head to turn away from the brightness. The three men walked back into the room and surrounded me.

"Ok, Andy" my interrogator began "I know who you are, why do you insist on pretending you are not Andy of MI6?"

"Ok" I replied in a calm voice "You know, but I really don't know what you want from me, I know nothing, I am such a tiny person in such a big organisation, I just follow orders, I do as they tell me, but they never tell me anything"

I lied, doing just as the training manual says. I wish I had experienced the fake kidnapping in England, I could have benefited so much from that experience.

"Andy, you have given up so quickly, the others took far longer to admit to me who they were"

"What others? I only know about myself, I don't know who you are talking about, I'm too small for them to tell me anything big like that" This was a more or less true statement, I knew I'd replaced an agent, but I knew nothing about the reason why.

"Tell me about Oleg, Andy"

"Oleg? Oleg who? I don't know any Oleg, I told you I know nothing, I am too small to be told anything, I just do as they order me"

Apparently, he thinks I know something because my answer gained me a seriously heavy punch to my left cheek. The blow jolting my head so violently I felt the muscles in my neck rip.

"Andy, I know you know Oleg, don't lie to me"

"Oleg who? I don't know any Oleg"

"You know Andy, tell me about him"

It hadn't occurred to me yet who he was asking about I really was answering honestly.

"I would love to tell you about Oleg, but you are not telling which Oleg, how can I tell you something when you don't tell me who you ask about"

Another punch to the same cheek, now this was starting to hurt.

"Andy, why do you want to make it difficult for yourself"

He grabbed my hair and slammed my face into the table, it didn't hurt at all as I managed to let my forehead take the hit.

"I know you know Oleg, Andy, why are you being so stupid, this is going to get a lot worse for yourself"

"Why are you not listening to me? I do not know any Oleg, I think you deliberately ask me questions you know I can't answer just so you can hurt me. It's not necessary, I will tell you, but you should ask me questions I know the answer to. I want to tell you"

"Why are you here in Angola Andy?"

"Working for UN Security Council resolution 626" I replied honestly, in an attempt to show I would answer questions I knew answers to.

My answer earned me another punch to the same cheek, it didn't hurt much more now, but my neck couldn't take the strain and I felt it crack, I'd torn a muscle.

"You are here to spy on the Russians Andy, the UN is just a cover for you, see I know who you are" One of the other men grabbed my shoulders and tipped me back on the chair, I fell backwards I couldn't stop the fall to the floor. The two men that had been quiet until now gave me a thorough kicking to my body, legs and head. I tried to get into a foetal position, curled up to protect myself from some of the blows. Kicks to my broken rib hurt most, I couldn't catch my breath as each time I breathed in and out it felt as though the rib was pushing into my lungs. They finished with the kicking and lifted me back into the chair at the table and stood behind me.

"I am here to observe the withdrawal of Cuban military, everyone knows Russians are supplying the Cubans, so obviously whatever you supply the Cubans needs to be confirmed it leaves the country according to the agreements."

"That's not such a big secret is it Andy, you are what you say, and that is nothing. I know why you are here, I want to know about Oleg"

"Who the fuck is Oleg!?" I screamed still totally mystified by the line of questioning.

"You know Oleg, you have talked to him, tell me what he said to you. Tell me where he is living now."

"I am trying to think who Oleg is, I never heard this name before"

"I know you drove him to a safe location in the south of England, why you didn't tell me this, so I know you are not telling me everything you know" Now it dawned on me, Oleg Gordievsky is the Russian double agent I drove from the safe house to Fork Monckton. There must be an MI6 mole telling them every detail, this shouldn't be common knowledge to anyone.

"I would tell you if I know something, I want to answer your questions"

My reply earned me another serious beating by the two goons behind me. The pain is hard to describe, once you get to a certain level it doesn't feel as though it can hurt anymore, so I just curled up into a ball and let the kicks and punches pour into me, there's nothing else you can do.

"Andy, I just told you I know you drove Oleg Gordievsky, you spent time with him, what do you know? You can tell me and the pain may stop for you"

"I don't know any Oleg Gord... Gordev..., I didn't catch the name you just said, I don't remember him, when was this you say?"

I didn't have anything I could tell, I drove him for a few hours. Gordievsky was sat in the back of the car with armed officers and another in the front with me driving. I spoke to him, yes, but only chit chat.

"I don't remember this person, if you know who I am you know I just do photocopying, I am nothing, and I know nothing, I wish I could tell you what you want to know, they don't tell me anything". This line of conversation was going nowhere, he must surely know that, what did he think I could tell him? Gordievsky was not my agent, I wasn't the one getting information from Gordievsky.

"You lie Andy, you just lie"

With that I took a really brutal beating from the two tough guys next to me, I could feel the pain was beginning to take its toll on my body. I'm not a trained soldier, I was quite fit from the sport that I did, but I wasn't hardened like a soldier, it wouldn't take long for these guys to beat me to death.

"Stop" I yelled, "Ok, what can I tell you" I was hoisted back into the chair at the table.

"Where did you take him?"

"I don't remember, I'm not employed to remember things, I just make photocopies, you have bad information on me.

If I drove this person, it must have been years ago, I don't remember anyone by that name, please, believe me, I am trying to help myself and you, I want to answer your questions, but I honestly do not know the answers to your questions. Please stop hurting me" I sounded pathetic, the kicks and punches were nothing compared to what I knew these men will do to me soon if I don't give them something. "Can you remind me who this person is? I do not recall him at all"

"You took Gordievsky from Russia, you know who I talk of Andy, and you took him to a place to be safe. Tell me where you took him"

"I have never been to Russia, you have the wrong person I am sorry." It was true I never have visited Russia.

"No Andy, I didn't say YOU drove him from Russia, you took him from a safe house in England and I need you to tell me where he is now. I tell you what Andy, how about I leave you with my two friends here for a while, maybe they can jog your memory"

"No, wait, help me to remember, what year was this supposed to happen because I do not know Oleg Gordi .... Whatever his name" I pretended not to know the surname.

"1982 Andy you know that. Don't belittle yourself, I know who you are, you are important to MI6, stop playing games Andy, I'm getting bored by your pretence"

"Ok, let me think, in 1982, it was the end of the Falklands War, yes, I was involved in a minor way with that conflict, I was never part of any other work at that time" I was trying to keep him talking in the room, I didn't want him to leave I knew I'd be getting a good kicking if he did. I also knew the date he gave me was the wrong one, Gordievsky escaped to England in 1985, was this false information as some kind of trap. Anyhow, I'd use the error, if that is what it was, as a way to pretend I did not know Oleg and to try to keep my interrogator thinking I had no idea who Oleg Gordievsky was. I doubt it was working but I had to try every trick I could think of under the circumstances, and it wasn't easy to think clearly.

"I was busy helping to trace Exocet missiles in the year 1982 until the war ended in June that year. I had no other work, it was all I was concerned with at that time." I kept talking to keep him in the room "Are you sure it was 1982 if you think I am involved with this person as you say"

The interrogation went back and forth for ages maybe a few hours, I lost track of time, I knew it was still daylight. I tried to keep his interest, but I told him nothing about Gordievsky, as I had nothing to tell, there was little I could do to add any information where I had none. After a while, I tried a different tack.

"I wonder if you can help me, I have been hurt by you guys, I need water, maybe a little food, with some rest maybe it will help me remember"

"No, Andy you don't get food or water, I am not going to waste it on you. You will sit here until you tell me what I wish to know". Clearly, knowing where Gordievsky was living was important to him, I guessed they plan to assassinate him. The good news was, they had no idea where he was living. With that, all three men left the room. To my mind this was going nowhere, I had no information I could give regarding Gordievsky, and these people will soon get fed up asking. Then what next?

As they left the room, I noticed as they closed the door there didn't seem to be any kind of lock. Most unusual for a prison cell, maybe this room wasn't normally used for that. I waited a few moments before I went to the door, listened carefully. I could not hear any sound that indicated to me there was a guard near the door. I slowly and quietly turned the door handle, the door opened, I let it open just the smallest crack. I smelt the fresh air, I slowly moved the door wider. The door let out a little creak noise as I tried to look outside. Suddenly a black guy, he must have been sitting to one side just a few feet away, leapt up from his seat and started to shout in chokwe at me. He had a rifle in his arms which he pointed at me, he grabbed the door, opened it fully and gave me a huge whack on the head with the barrel end. I put my hands up, backing away I kept staring at him, another bloke came running in and there was a massive din as they shouted and hit me repeatedly with their guns. I retreated to the chair, telling them to calm down, I was just looking for water. The other three white men came running back into the room and all five of them gave me a thorough beating, kicking and punching. I just kept repeating Ok, ok, ok as the blows kept coming. Almost unconscious now the blows stopped but with one of the men holding me down in the chair. The man that had been doing all the talking left the room while the others stood guard over me. Every part of my body was in pain, so much pain, I was feeling very weak and faint, I was thinking it would be better for them to end my life now.

After a minute or two the guy in charge came back into the room and spoke "Andy, you think we would just leave the door open for you to walk out, what an idiot you are", I couldn't disagree with him, "I will stop you walking about when I don't give you permission to." I was expecting to be tied to the chair, what happened was worse of course. He had in his hand a hammer and a couple of nails, about three inches long, two of the men grabbed my wrist and held it onto the table in front of me with my fingers held out straight, he pushed one of the nails into the back of my hand and hammered it into the table, I screamed, although I don't know why. Compared to the beatings it didn't hurt that much. My other wrist was placed onto the table and this was also nailed to the tabletop. This was not a good position to be in. From now on, any punches or beatings were going to seriously damage my hands as I moved about, I needed to try to keep my hands still.

"Andy, you told me you wanted to tell me everything you know about Gordievsky, you can sit there for as long as it takes, we will see if you remember anything more." With that, all of them left me alone in the room again.

This was not turning out to be a fun day out in the sun. By some miracle, I could feel nothing had been seriously damaged by the nails passing through my hands, the exit of the nails through my hands was really hurting but nothing more than I had already felt from the beatings I had received.

Psychologically, it was hell, the feeling of helplessness and vulnerability was overwhelming, I started to shake, which I tried to control. I knew if they kicked me or dragged me around my hands would be ripped apart. It was a very uncomfortable experience. I sat and thought if there could be any story I could make up to give him what they wanted from me. But then what? The only end to this would be my death, it couldn't be anything else now.

I sat alone for hours and it started to get dark. Nothing was happening, no more interrogations took place. I couldn't move and it was getting very uncomfortable not being able to move at all. I did try to shuffle the chair back a little so that I could rest my head on my arms, which was more comfortable. I cannot describe how much pain I was in, I couldn't breathe properly, my jaw hurt, my neck and especially my hands, they were now very painful. Of course, there was no way I could get any sleep like this.

I sat there all night, I occasionally heard movement and talking outside I was on an army camp after all. I began to see light start to glow around the door and blacked-out windows and the sounds of people waking and moving. What would this new day bring me? As the sun got brighter, my eyes accustomed to the dark I could see around the room. There was nothing except the table and chairs one of which I was sat on. I felt so alone and I was shaking from the pain.

Maybe an hour later, I heard an unusual sound, a distant engine drone, it was getting nearer. An aeroplane! A small light aircraft, single-engine. I heard the engine slow as it made all the noises of landing at the runway just a hundred yards away. I heard it taxi and park somewhere not too far away.

This seemed to make a few people in this camp get a little more mobile, there was some shouting, I couldn't make out what it was, mostly chokwe I think. The engine of the plane stopped, I couldn't hear much more other than the excitement in the camp. Suddenly I heard footsteps in the dirt outside my hut and shouting. The door burst open, it was my interrogator again, oh no here we go again more pain! I saw he was carrying the hammer, this didn't look good for me at all. He was followed by three black guys with guns.

"Andy, you are no use." With that, he grabbed one of my arms at the wrist and used the claw of the hammer to wrench the nail from one hand then the other. I can't tell you how much it hurt, I screamed as the hammer pressed hard into the back of my hands to lever out the nails, I screamed and screamed loud, it was uncontrollable, I couldn't help myself. He commanded the three black guys something in chokwe, I assume it was to tie my hands and to take me out of the room, as that is what they did. They weren't very good at tying the rope around my wrists with my hands behind my back, although they pulled it tight, I felt it loosen when they let it go. I was kicked on the backside to make me move. Maybe the arrival of the plane at the airfield had spooked them, I don't know, but more than a coincidence that it arrived and then suddenly I was being marched outside. They did seem to be panicking and excited by the plane.

With one black guy in front of me and two behind, I was pushed to the door where more shoves indicated I should turn right once I was outside, then right and right again between the buildings. The white men stayed in the camp, finished with me, this was it, this was going to be my end. We headed behind the buildings and toward the woods where I had circled the camp yesterday morning. The black men chatting in chokwe, I had no idea what they were talking about, but I could tell they were still high and drunk from the night before. We walked parallel to the runway, I dare not turn to look around, I knew it would result in more blows from the AK47's they each had. I noticed the weapons looked quite new, not the old badly maintained weapons I had seen on the journey here. They were being supplied with fresh equipment, not preparing to cease hostilities as they should be. We walked across the north-south road from the village that also crossed the runway. The guys escorting me laughing and joking as we walked, occasionally hitting me in my back or head with their weapons, sometimes it would be a kick. I just followed the man in front into the woods. I knew now I was going to be killed here, they were just taking me far enough away so that the stench of my rotting body couldn't be smelt from the camp, I'm sure there are animals around that would enjoy my flesh for breakfast. As we walked I desperately tried to think how to escape, there was nothing I could do, it's not like me to not give it a go, but I really couldn't see a way out of this. Surrounded by the men guarding me, hands tied behind my back, no food or water for 24 hours in this heat, badly beaten, I was not in any place to put up a fight.

After walking for a few minutes, I guessed about 400 to 500 yards inside the woods and in plenty of cover, we came to a very small clearing, the place stunk. Either they had killed here before or it was the place where they disposed of the toilet waste, it wasn't pleasant at all. My blood-stained shirt collar was grabbed from behind jerking me to a halt. I was shoved back to stand against a tree, I leaned back against it, I don't know why it just seemed to be better that way for some reason. I instantly regretted it. As my hands rested on the tree trunk almost immediately an insect bit my hand at the base of my thumb. This caused me to try to shake it off, a pointless reaction as I was about to be shot. Come on you arseholes get on with it, I hoped they were capable of shooting straight to make my end quick. The men that had walked me here, stood for a few moments finishing their cigarettes and chattering among themselves, moving very slow in their morning hungover state. As I shook the pesky biting insect off my hand, I felt the badly tied rope around my hands become even looser. I could slip my hands out of the knot. I didn't let the rope drop to the floor, the men may see that I was free. I held it in my hand, I was definitely free of it. If I didn't do something in the next second I was going to be dead. I didn't want to die today. I wanted to see my wife Julie and my daughter Joanne again. In that one second it dawned on me that I had had quite a good life so far, I'd done and achieved many things, I'd been offered a privileged career almost no one else ever had, I'd married and bought a house, my daughter was just a few weeks old, and I wanted to see her grow up.

This was it, the men started to ready themselves, they threw away their cigarettes after extinguishing the tiny stub, and started to prepare their weapons to use on me. I stood staring at them wondering how much more pain I'd suffer today, would my end be quick, or would they leave me half alive, so that I felt the animals rip bits off me, eating me alive. I hoped they would do the job properly. The guns were being cocked, a bullet in each rifle chamber was intended for me, these men really did look a ragtag bunch. Let's go, let's do it, do it now!

With that and without any great thought, I lifted one foot against the tree trunk and gave a huge push, now I ran with my hands completely free, I ran straight at them, only about ten feet away from where I was stood against the tree. I ran at them and right through them, passing them close enough to barge one guy on the shoulder causing him to stumble, he was taken by surprise, my charge was like a rugby player running to score a try. I ran through their untidy line of three and kept going. The weight of their weapons was a disadvantage to them. It took a vital half-second for them to realise what was happening by which time I'd covered at least six feet past them. The men with their heavy guns were slow to spin around to aim at me, I hoped if they were stupid enough they'd fire a shot too early and shoot each other as they turned around to where I was now running and running fast. I zig-zagged through the trees, I needed to get some distance between us, enough to try to get some trees between me and them. It seemed ages before the first shot was fired in my direction. Taken completely by surprise, the men started firing, what seemed a good three or four seconds after I ran through their line. I don't know where the first bullets went, probably fired in panic rather than aimed, the rounds disappeared into the trees somewhere. The next shots felt closer as they gathered their senses to the situation. I heard and felt the shock waves as they zinged past me. I don't know if they were chasing me or standing still to fire their guns, I wasn't going to waste time turning to look, I just kept going full pelt, adrenalin assisting my dash, and I felt plenty of it surging into my body. The shots were getting closer, shattering trees and branches around me. My shirt burst forward as one bullet passed between my left arm and my body, so close it took some skin away from my rib cage, it stung, but right now it didn't bother me at all. I ran to put more trees for cover between me and the three-man firing squad, I have no idea if I was breathing or holding my breath, anticipating a bullet into my back at any moment, but so far the men's aim was very poor. From the sound of the guns firing at me, I must have extended my lead away from them by maybe thirty yards, with plenty of trees between me and them, I could hear shouting, yeh, like I'm going to stop because you ask me to, I thought to myself. I really had an advantage now, I had some distance, while they had to carry and fire weapons weighing seven pounds each, holding them would slow their attempt to run after me. I kept running the guns sounding further and further behind.

I had done it, I escaped!

24. On The Run

I didn't want to celebrate too early, I had run from the firing squad, and they were still shooting at me, I knew I could make it back to somewhere safe if I kept going. I kept running even though my lungs were fit to burst, my legs were burning, I had not had any food or drink for 24 hours in the heat of Angola, I had been badly beaten for 24 hours and my hands were injured from the nails hammered through them. But I was alive right now and I was going to do my utmost to stay that way.

Running through the woods away from the three men chasing me, away from the army camp on the other side of the road behind me. What to do next, where do I go? One place to head for would be to the camp back at Filipe Lomba's house. Would it be safe, would the soldiers from the camp be heading there knowing I might try to get there myself? There was little choice it was my only option, that or dying in the scrub-land of Angola, no food, no water. I decided, as I ran, that was where I'd head. Maybe, I thought that the three men would claim they had killed me rather than face being punished if they admitted to their failure. That was a long shot, everyone would have heard the shooting. I made a wide sweep slowly turning right, a big enough loop so that the men running after me would not see me and gain on me by cutting the curve short. The firing was dying down, maybe they had run out of bullets, maybe they had realised I had got away and it was futile shooting at trees. Either way, they would be heading back to the army camp and report I had escaped. Then they would all be after me, I needed to get back to Filipe's house and my UN group fast. I wondered if the UN group had heard the shooting.

Running through the woods, I felt relatively safe from mines, I doubted any would have been laid here, mostly they were in open fields, I kept running, the years as a child spending so much time tracking animals taught me how to move smoothly and quietly, to leave little trace as I ran, to avoid breaking any twigs to give away my path. I wasn't as swift as I could be, due to my bruises and it was very difficult running with a broken rib, I could not catch my breath properly, but the pain I could handle, I have a very high pain threshold. Now I was sure the adrenalin that was surging through my body was now giving me super strength. Pure fear was pushing me on more than any normal being, my eyes were more alert than they would be without the tiredness and injuries in normal life. Adrenalin is a marvellous thing, right now it was keeping me alive for sure.

I ran in a big curve, for about two miles in the woods, I was, at last, heading back to Lumbala village, but of course, this also meant I was getting close to the army camp too. I had no choice, it was the best and only way to try to get out of here. I would surely die trying to go anywhere else, I just had to hope the NPLA, Cubans or Russians were not waiting for me in the village, would they think I'd come back toward them?

The runway would be on my right-hand side somewhere, I had my bearings, using the sun, at this time of the early morning, I guessed about 8 am, it was still relatively low and usable for direction, I didn't stop running, and I didn't want the adrenalin energy to end just yet. I needed it to keep me going. I could see to my left the woods were thinning out, so I turned more right, I should be heading slightly south and west now, and the village will be getting closer. Eventually, after maybe twenty minutes running, with breathing almost impossible, I had no choice, I needed to stop, I crouched down in the trees to keep low, I could not hear anything, no shooting, no shouting, no unusual noises indicating someone was tracking me, just birds and noises of the jungle. To my left was a sloping bank down, maybe if I dropped down it I would gain some more cover, I walked over and slid down, finding that at the bottom of the bank was a road. I would be me more exposed on the road, but my pathway would be easier, I'd hear anyone approaching by car. I moved cautiously at first, then started to run once I had enough oxygen in my lungs. The road was heading straight back to the village.

About half a mile on the road, about four minutes running I started to see signs of the village ahead, I couldn't see any movement or any people searching for me. I passed by a few houses where there were few people about, I felt sure they were friendly villagers and not the NPLA troops, but I had to be careful, I didn't want to cause a stir. After a very short time, I saw the road ahead joining the main road we had driven along from the Zambezi River into the village, I recognised where I was and Filipe's house was just a few hundred yards dead ahead. The cover from the woods was almost gone now and at the road junction where there was a triangular island formed by the road junction turning left and right and a rough football pitch on the right, where the kids would be playing in their new football shirts soon.

To the north was the army camp, straight-ahead Filipe and my UN group would be waiting, I had no plan what to tell them, where I had been, I would just tell them we need to go immediately. At the junction, there were a couple of villagers, I had seen them the night before dancing in celebration of the football shirts.

They looked at me, clearly able to see I was covered in blood, they waved me across the road in a gesture to indicate it was safe to cross, then they continued on their way, not stopping to help me more. I knew why, it was good they did that one little thing to help me cross the road safely, but any more than that they would surely be getting themselves into my bad business. I understood why they could not help me more. They knew I was in trouble and the best way for them to help was to help me cross the road to get to Filipe and my group.

I ran across the road and down the narrow street to the gate and walled garden belonging to Filipe. Behind it would be the vehicles and people of my group, we'd jump into our cars and leave before trouble arrived from the camp just a few hundred yards away. I got to the gate, pausing slightly to listen for sounds inside the garden. There were none. I could hear Filipe talking in his kitchen in his loud African voice. Safety at last. But the vehicles and tents of the UN and my people had gone. Not a sign of them. I dashed across the garden to the kitchen door and burst in.

Inside Filipe was talking to a man, I had not seen him before, I stopped abruptly at the door wondering whether I should turn and run again. Filipe put his hand out to me. "Anselmo, my friend, come in quickly. Oh my, you look a mess. Your people left yesterday after you went missing, they were frightened of the army camp. They left your bag for you, here it is on the table. They thought it would be the best thing to do as they had no defence against the army. What has happened to you?"

"I have no time to explain," I said, "I need to get out of here fast, the NPLA and some Russians are trying to kill me. I escaped from them and now they must be searching for me. I think they may come here very soon. May I have some water please?" There were small cloth bags and money on the kitchen table, they were obviously in the middle of doing a deal with the latest diamonds that Filipe and his people had mined.

"This gentleman is Victor. He is my diamond buyer. He came here in his aeroplane this morning. I think you should go with him, he will fly you somewhere safe, if you can make it to the airfield"

That explained the noise of an aeroplane I heard landing earlier today. The airstrip was dangerously close to the army camp. I thought it a bad idea to try to get to the plane right next to the camp. But, it was my only way out. My cars had gone, it was a long drive back to Luena and the camp there. It was a good risk if Victor agreed.

"Is the plane ready to go, is it fuelled, I can't hang around, they are looking for me, they will be here in minutes I am sure"

Victor spoke, he had an accent I wasn't entirely familiar with. Maybe South American, but not Spanish, so I guessed he may be Brazilian. A lot of business was done with Brazil, the countries have the same Portuguese heritage. "Yes, I have refuelled it, as soon as Filipe and I have concluded our business, we can go. We should be five minutes."

"No", I replied "We cannot be seen together, they will kill you too if we are together. I will grab my bag, and go now to the airfield and hide until you arrive, please be quick." I would thank Filipe for his help later, right now there was no time.

"Ok" Victor agreed "You get to my plane, it is locked, take the keys, hide in the back, I will be there as fast as I can, we can take off right away, it's ready to go"

I reached out to Filipe to shake his hand, he looked down at the blood-stained mess it was and pulled his hand back. "Go, Anselmo, no time for goodbyes, we will talk again sometime soon I am sure. Take this water and some bread and fruit" He stuffed it into my bag for me. I realised my hands are stiffening up and not very mobile. Adrenalin still holding back the pain. I slung my kit bag over my shoulders "Thank you my friend" I said looking him in the eye to transfer my genuine thanks to him.

As I spoke, we all jumped at the sound of approaching vehicles coming down the road toward the house, they were 50 yards away. "Go this way Anselmo, to the back of the house." Filipe's wife was in the corridor that led to the back of the house, "Come I will show you" she waved me urgently down the corridor to a back door into the garden. Filipe and Victor started to gather up their business off the table. As I reached the door and disappeared through it, I gave my thanks to Filipe's wife. "Thank you so much for your kind help. I am sorry to bring this trouble to your home"

25. My First Solo Flight

"Go, go, go" she ushered me out the door and closed it behind me to help provide cover from the angry men now shouting at the front door, vehicles piling through the gate into the garden just the other side of the house.

I ran keeping the house for cover between me and the angry-sounding men. I dived over the four feet high inner wall. Keeping low, I turned right and ran crouching to the north toward the plane. Reaching the outer garden wall, which was much higher, there was a small gate through to the outside, it was unlocked and I disappeared through it to the outside. I could hear lots of angry shouting from the house. Filipe was in trouble now, there was nothing I could do to help him, and I was in full flight mode. Between me and the airfield was another house, I ran across the open ground and used it for cover. I began to hear shots firing. Oh my god, they were killing Filipe and his wife and most probably Victor too. I had to move fast now, they would come for me for sure, but did they know which way I was heading, would they guess I would be running toward the airfield and their camp just a few yards the other side of it.

I ran to the edge of the airstrip, I could see the Cessna small aircraft just the other side of the runway, parked next to the refuelling barrels, but right next to the first buildings of the army camp. I was going to be lucky to get to the plane undetected. I could hear more shots and Filipe's wife screaming behind me. The sound spurred me on, I dashed across the open runway sure that the house and walls that I had just come from would give me a little cover from the crazy men shooting innocent people behind me. I was sure Victor would be dead too, my pilot, but I still had every intention of making it to the aeroplane right in front of me. I got to the door on the pilot side of the plane. Quickly unlocked the door and shoved the keys into the ignition slot on the lower edge of the flight deck. I threw my bag across to the passenger seat on the right of the cockpit and jumped into the pilot seat, in my total fear of what was happening behind me, adrenalin had returned and I felt no pain from my hands or bruised body as I swung into the seat. I turned the key and master switch on and heard the gyros begin to wind up to speed. I had no idea what my plan was, but I was pretty sure I knew enough from my four flying lessons a few years ago that I could get this plane started and off the ground, then I would figure what to do and where to go. For now, I was running on fear and I wanted to get this plane to fly me out of here. The plane was a Cessna 172 that I had flown before, I was familiar with the layout and start-up procedure, although I skipped all the pre-flight checks. No time to hesitate or be cautious here.

I slid the pilot seat forward so I could reach the pedals. Once the gyros had got up to speed I saw the fuel tanks were showing full on the gauge. I pumped the primer on the left three times for a cold start, I left all the light switches off so as not to attract attention to myself, my head was working at triple speed trying to think of everything I needed to do to get this thing running and into the air. So far no one has noticed me sitting in the aeroplane, of course, I had no idea how long before they would. I set the mixture slider in, and the throttle control at one eighth in, ready to start. This was it, what else did I need to do, I didn't want or have time to fail my start.

I hadn't put my seat belt on deliberately just in case they started to fire at me while sitting here or taxiing, I could jump out in a hurry, I'd put it on later. The doors were closed. I turned the key to start and the engine easily burst into life, which was a surprise I didn't expect it to be this easy. I felt confident I could get into the air now. I set the handbrake off and pushed the throttle forward to start moving. I wasn't going to waste time taxiing to the end of the runway, I'd go from here. In my bag I had the camera provided by the UN, the camera I used earlier was my own SIS camera, I had two for the different types of pictures I knew I would be taking. The camera I used yesterday morning had been taken from me when I had been grabbed by the Russians. I pulled the zip on my bag open and quickly rummaged for the camera and found it easily. As I began to move with one hand I took a snap of the camp to my left and dropped the camera into my lap to take more pictures in a few seconds. I controlled the plane to the middle of the runway and pushed the throttle fully in for take-off. As the plane picked up speed I pulled the flap lever down for 10-degree flaps and let the plane pick up speed while keeping it in the centre of the runway. A quick scan of the instruments showed they were all working fine, airspeed active, engine temperature coming up to normal. Looking out the front of the plane I saw there was plenty of runway left, even though I had started my run one third down the runway. As the airspeed indicator reached the green section at 50 knots I let the speed gain another 5 knots before easing back on the yoke to get the plane off the ground. The bumpy ground was getting smoother as the lift generated by the wings softened the bumps. One second later the plane left the ground, I grabbed the camera in my lap and without looking in the viewfinder took a snap of the army camp to my left.

Fig. 5 As I took off it was pure luck this photograph came out as it did, the arrow in the picture showing the door of the room where I was held captive.

I looked to the right, I saw something that would haunt me for the rest of my life. I saw the NPLA soldiers swarming around Filipe's house, just outside the door to the house laying in the most awkward position on his front was Filipe, a puddle of blood on the floor, he had been shot dead. A few feet away Victor laying on his back I guessed he had a similar end, as the plane moved on I got a quick view through the front door of the house, I could see the feet of Filipe's wife as she was laying in the doorway. I felt sick that I had caused this to happen to them, this happy man and his wife, who were so kind to us were now lying dead on the floor of their house. The soldiers below saw the plane taking off and fired a few shots at me before it was clear to them the target was too fast and difficult to hit.

My problem now was where to go. I kept the plane low and turned left away from the danger I had just left behind. It only dawned on me now, what I had done. I've taken off in a type of plane and that I have had only four hours flying experience. I have no pilots licence, no idea where I'm going, or to that matter, when I get there, little idea how I get this thing down safely. After settling the plane into cruise mode, flaps up, throttle eased back a little it was time to think clearly. I reached into my bag and found the water bottle and took a big swig from it. I tossed the camera onto the seat to my right. Should I head south or west into Zambia? I don't know any airfields there and so far I hadn't found any map in the plane. North? This east side of Angola was the most hostile I didn't think it was a good option. So I'd fly west, in that direction I could try to find my way back to Luena, it was a larger airport and the UN had a camp where my group were probably headed right now in the cars. I could re-join them, give them some bullshit story that I'd figure out shortly. It seemed like a plan, not a good plan, but then nothing about my situation was good right now. I turned left and headed west keeping low for now as I would still be in range of the surface to air missiles I'd seen in the Lumbala army camp. I guessed they would have a range of up to 10 miles, given I had flown in the wrong direction for three minutes I calculated in ten minutes in this direction I'd be safe. Could they prepare and fire a SAM missile in less than 10 minutes? I had no idea, I'd keep flying low for a while and I will find out for sure. Would they be so bothered to waste a missile on me? Who knows, I wasn't going to want to find out in this little old plane. Next problem was, how far could I fly, what was my range? I guessed I could make it to Luena easily it was about 200 miles as the crow flies, I'd still be careful to fly efficiently as I didn't yet know where the airfield was exactly, and it may take me several attempts to land successfully.

After 10 minutes I guessed I was now relatively safe. I felt sure someone would be watching me on radar, but as this was Victor's plane and he flew here all the time doing his business. I thought I stood a chance I'd be left alone. I decided now to climb, I increased throttle a little and gently gave a pull on the yoke and noticed the climb indicator raise to 300 feet per minute that will do until I reach 3000 feet. I checked all systems, eased the mixture slider back to get a better fuel rate, the temperature indicator rose a little so I didn't want to over weaken the mix too much. So far so good. Should I turn on the transponder and send out a squawk signal to identify myself, I decided not to do that until later when I'd squawk an emergency code to indicate I had a problem. I had no idea of any radio frequencies for the airfields here so I'd have to remember the emergency frequency for the radio too. There must be some kind of chart in the plane, I was sure Victor didn't fly without, I knew some bush pilots didn't use maps but at least they had them in the plane. I looked around felt under the seat maybe there was something under there, I found a pouch in it was a map folder of this area, at last, something to help me find my way. I looked at the map, there was no protractor to figure the compass heading I would need to fly to Luena. Looking at the map the rough direction would be 290 degrees, I was flying 270 so I turned right to 290 on the compass and direction indicator in front of me. At 3000 feet I eased the throttle back slightly to cruise at 120 knots and adjusted the trim to achieve level flight. Now I could relax a little and do some maths. Being so tired I found it hard to do the calculations necessary for my journey. 200 miles at 120 knots would take me how long before I reached Luena? 1 hour would be 120 miles leaving 80 more miles, the remaining 80 miles is three-quarter of an hour flying time. So I settled on one and three-quarter hours flying time. I rechecked, such a simple math problem was proving to be so difficult. I tried different ways to do the sum, each time I got 1.75 hours. I looked at the clock in front of me, it was now 08:13. Just before 10:00 I should see the city and I can find the airport and land. I took note of the time on the plane's clock.

I looked in my bag for the food Filipe had given me. I hadn't eaten for at least 27 hours now. I ate a banana and some bread and a good swig of water. I didn't think about rationing as I was only two hours at most from Luena and safety.

Now as I relaxed the adrenalin was disappearing from my body, every part of my body started to hurt. My hands hurt the most, it was really painful to hold the flight controls, my face was throbbing and a headache was starting. My rib wasn't so bad as long as I breathed in and out in shallow breaths, if I breathed out too deeply it felt like my rib was pressing into my diaphragm below my lungs and then it hurt. What had happened during the previous 24 hours, was now starting to dawn on me and I became quite emotional, the vision of seeing those three dead people who had done nothing wrong other than help me had given shelter to the UN team and provided food for us. The act of kindness had got Filipe and his wife killed, Victor had done nothing other than to be in the wrong place at the wrong time. It's an image and a feeling of guilt I will carry to the day I die. I wasn't sure at that point in time how I would cope with this once, if, I ever got home.

For now, I mustn't think negatively. I need to land this plane somewhere safely. I need to return to the UN, somehow blag my way to the British Embassy, not the Spanish it was time to lose my Anselmo Gil persona, I wasn't yet sure how I would do that. The embassies were in Luanda 700 miles away, we had flown from there to Luena in UN planes.

While the aeroplane cruised nicely at 3000 feet and 120 knots, I started to think. Who was the mole that gave me away to the Russians? I sat and went through the options. Only the people in that first meeting at the Reform Club in London would know I am here and who I was. Chris Curwen, "C", I didn't believe it could be him, I don't know why I ruled him out, treacherous moles can penetrate every level, I just didn't think it could be him.

Max, "C's" assistant, he would know everyone that Chris knew and where and when they would be places, it could be him, he has access to every secret file that was in "C's" office.

Roger, it was his plan, a bad plan, I had gone along with it, he couldn't be blamed entirely, I could have always refused to take on the mission. There was something about Roger that I, and indeed "C" was uncertain about, I remembered "C" asking me what I thought of Roger. He was an upper-class dick, with the proverbial silver spoon in his mouth, he had a manner about him that made myself and "C" question his abilities. He was smart enough to get me into place so quickly with all the necessary paperwork and character background I needed, I had to give that to him. But there was something about him that gave me the creeps, I could not say what it was, just a gut feeling.

Jean, she was a linguist and a good one, she would have some knowledge of who is doing what and where. I couldn't think that she would know enough secrets to act as an agent to the Russians, and she surely couldn't know I was in Lumbala yesterday, for now, I ruled her out.

Karen, my secretary. We had known each other for a long time now, we loved each other, if she was the mole then she could only pass on secrets on matters that only I had dealings with. Secretaries do not talk to each other on secret matters, I only ever heard them chat about clothes, makeup and men, just normal girlie stuff.

Who else knew about not only me but the others that had found an untimely end to their career? I pondered on this and started to let my mind drift into a daydream. The plane was flying straight and level it was easy to sit and not think too hard about flying the plane for a few moments. I formed some ideas and narrowed the list of suspects down to Roger and Max. I could not imagine anyone else would have enough knowledge of agents and their officers to get them killed.

What I thought would be an hour and twenty minutes into my flight, I started to look around for signs of the city of Luena. It was a big enough city it should be in plain view now. The land around was reasonably flat, yet so far no sign of it in mile after mile of scrubland. It should be here!

I set the transponder to 7700, the emergency squawk number to show air-traffic control I was in an emergency situation, I'd never set this piece of equipment before, my instructor had shown it to me and explained how it worked so this was my first time to set it. I also set the radio to 121.5 the emergency frequency that should be heard by any radio that communicated with aeroplanes. I called a Mayday on the radio but there was no reply, had I forgotten to do something? Am I transmitting? I went over the settings, everything seemed to be in order. Out of the window, I could see no sign of the city. I couldn't see any roads that might lead to the city. Where was I? I should be able to see the city. Had I drifted sideways in crosswinds so far that I was now miles off course? I looked at the chart again and again 290 degrees was the correct course to fly from Lumbala to Luena. I looked again at the clock it showed 10:33, I'd been flying 1 hour 20 minutes. NO. I'd been flying TWO hours 20 minutes. Shit, I must have drifted off into my daydream thinking I was half awake, but somehow I had fallen asleep while flying. SHIT, FUCK. The compasses showed I'd stayed on course, but I'd flown past the city in a doze. Oh what an idiot I am.

I took a swig of water and poured some over my head to wake myself up. Ok, what to do? Turn around and look for the city or keep going and aim directly for Luanda another 500 miles away. I looked at the fuel gauge. I knew the Cessna had a range of about 800 miles, in theory, I could make it to Luanda, but with little fuel to spare, I would not have many chances to make a good landing. I figured, if I kept going, even though it was much further, I would eventually see the coast and from there figure out where the city was. The coast would be the best landmark. Turning back onto a reciprocal flight path of 110 degrees, by now I could be miles out and completely miss Luena again. Right or wrong I decided to go for Luanda. At that city at least was the main UN base or better still the British Embassy. I still had water, some little food, and the shock of missing the entire city had injected more adrenalin back into my body and I was wide awake again, and my pains had disappeared into the background. I was going for Luanda.

26. Landing My First Solo Flight

I shifted in my seat, realised I still didn't have my seat belt on so I buckled up. Thinking about Health and Safety even in my situation did bring a little chuckle to myself. I found a new comfortable position in my seat and went over the plane's systems to check and recheck I was on course and calculated I would have enough fuel to make it to Luanda, but not much more. Tiredness was a concern, I'd already fallen asleep, I couldn't do that again. I opened the window next to me to get some air, but feeling the turbulence it caused inside the cockpit I thought this may use up more fuel with the extra drag, so after a minute or two, I shut it again. I found switches for cabin heat and cooling. I was now comfortable and ready to continue my long journey.

Time to do some more calculations. From Lumbala it was 700 miles to Luanda, a total of about 6 hours flying time. I'd been flying now for 2 and a half hours, so I had another 3 and a half hours to fly. Fuel flow rate according to the gauge was 7 gallons per hour. 7 x 6 hours = 42 gallons from full. I'd used 2.5 hours at 7 per hour 17.5 gallons already, leaving me, 24.5 gallons. At 7 gallons per hour, multiplied by 3.5 hours flight remaining, that's 24.5 gallons needed to fly to Luanda. Oh my goodness, I was only just going to make it. If I didn't get lost I'd be landing with only fumes remaining in the fuel tank. I had to find Luanda first time, find the airfield and land first attempt. Was this the correct decision? I don't know, I was too tired and in too much pain to think clearly. I tried the mixture slider to see if I could get any better fuel consumption without raising the engine temperature too much. The oil temperature was ok. I adjusted the mixture and settled for a compromise mix, lean, but not so lean to overheat the engine. The sound of the engine was on the edge of lumpy, I'd forget climbing and using more fuel, and hoped the wind direction was assisting me, I had no way to tell. I could feel the flight was flat and smooth. Nerves kicked in a little and with the pain and all I started to shake a little. I took another swig of water, I had a few pieces of fruit and bread left I'd save those for later.

I left the transponder on 7700 and double-checked it was turned on to indicate I was in distress to any Air Traffic Controller. Radio was set to 121.5 to listen and speak on the emergency frequency.

Three hours is a long time to sit and fly a plane alone. I was sure my nerves and adrenalin would give me some boost but I had to stay awake, not drift off into a sleep again, that would be a huge mistake. I sat back if it were possible in this situation, I was pleased with myself I had remembered so much from so few lessons. I wondered if I would be in trouble for flying without a licence, but at the end of the day, I had more to worry about. Time began to pass slowly, I looked around to see if there were any cities with runways within sight. I could see none, even though the weather was good and clear. Looking at the chart I was not going to fly over any towns for the entire journey. This was it, my first solo flight, and I'm flying without any real idea where I'm going other than the rough calculations I'd done in my tired bruised head.

I took a few moments to look at my hands and other injuries. My hands were covered in dry blood and hurt like crazy, a little stiff but not too bad. The nails had passed through both hands cleanly without damaging any bones, muscles or tendons, I think everything important must have been pushed aside as they passed through. The rest of me was just major bruising and nothing was broken apart from one rib and one tooth, as far as I could tell. My head was thumping hard, I think that was pure tiredness. I wasn't sure why I was shaking, maybe shock or nerves. I was sure I could make this journey as long as I stayed awake.

As I flew toward what I hoped would be the coast, somewhere there would be Luanda or another city nearby with an airfield, I tried to recall how to make a mayday call on the radio. On my sailing courses, I learnt the mnemonic MIPDANIO to help remember the order of the mayday message. I was so tired I couldn't remember everything I needed to report. I hoped that the aeronautical version was the same, but this should be enough for air traffic control if they received my distress call I was going to send soon.

M – Mayday

I – Identification,

P – Position,

D – Distress type,

A – Assistance required,

N – Number of people on board,

I – I could not recall what this was, I hoped it stood for Intention

O – I had absolutely no idea what the 'O' stood for, I could not recall at all. But I was sure the item at the end of the list was less important, so I wasn't going to let that worry me more than I was already. I rehearsed in my head what I was going to say. Initially, I'd keep it short and expand when asked.

Time passed so slowly, but finally, on the horizon, I could see the coast and the blue South Atlantic Sea beyond. My fuel gauges were all but empty. I put the headphones over my ears and I tried a call on the radio.

"Mayday, mayday, mayday, this is unknown call sign Cessna 172, heading 290 degrees, height 3000. Any call sign please acknowledge." There was no response, shit! I couldn't be lost still, there was the coast in front of me. Luanda has to be here somewhere. I repeated my call.

"Mayday, mayday, mayday, this is unknown call sign Cessna 172, heading 290 degrees, height 3000. Any call sign please acknowledge." With that, I heard a voice in the headphones.

"Unknown call sign this is Luanda air traffic control, I understand you are calling mayday, please confirm your situation"

"Mayday, I am a Cessna 172, I am transmitting squawk 7700, unknown position, probably to your south-east, I am injured, injuries not likely to be fatal. I am on zero fuel. I need vectors to Luanda Airport for landing any runway please, I am one sole on board. Over"

My stomach tied itself in knots with the sound of the voice on the radio. Happy I was being monitored and scared shit-less that very soon I would have to land this plane. I can't explain my feelings fully at that moment. I was going to make it, yet danger was still to come.

"Roger, Cessna 172. Understood you have injuries and you are one sole aboard, stand by, I see you on radar 17 miles south-east of Luanda airfield, standby for directions. You will have priority Runway 05 left"

"Thank you, I need every assistance to land please. I request British Embassy staff to be present on my landing. Repeat I request British Embassy staff. I am code Madrid, Cessna 172"

"Cessna 172, I do not understand code Madrid, please confirm"

"Please convey the message to British Embassy that I am code Madrid"

Madrid was my code name. I used this to inform Embassy staff who I am and that I should be afforded official diplomatic status, but it did tell anyone listening that I was someone from the intelligence community, and the British were not supposed to be active in this country. It was slightly foolish to say this on open radio, but I felt I had no choice. I didn't want to be arrested for stealing an aircraft and flying without a licence.

"Cessna 172 Roger, please continue on your current course and flight level"

I had no idea if he understood my message, but if he passed it to the Embassy in Luanda it should be enough to get help from them.

As we spoke the city came into view in the hazy sunlight. I was perfectly on course I could not believe it. The low fuel buzzer started to sound.

"Cessna 172 will continue on course and await landing instructions. I have zero fuel, I need straight in instructions please" The buzzing fuel gauge became a very annoying noise.

"Cessna 172, do you understand how to turn and fly to bearings I give you." I guessed he asked the question because I had asked for every assistance to land.

"I understand, I can fly to your directions. I can control speed and height. Cessna 172"

"Understood Cessna 172, standby for instructions" How long was this going to take them to get me down. I guessed the ATC controller was seeking advice, and I hoped he was passing the message to the British Embassy.

"Cessna 172, expect instructions to land runway 05 left, continue on 290 degrees and descend to 2000. Are you able to comply?"

"Roger, 290 and descending to 2000. Speed currently 120"

A new voice came on the radio. I thought this would be someone that can give me instructions on how to land such as another pilot.

"Hello Cessna 172, this is Luanda airfield ATC. I am a qualified pilot, I am informed of your situation and I will help you land safely, I assure you I will do my best to get you down safely. What is your name?"

"Thank you, my name is Andy. I have zero fuel I will have only one attempt at a landing, let's make it a good one. I have four hours previous flying experience, and I have just flown 6 hours to Luanda. I am one sole on board. I have injuries, but not life-threatening, I can control the plane, thank you in advance for your help"

"Ok, understood Cessna 172. Your message is being conveyed to the British Embassy as we speak. Now I require you to slow to 80 knots are you able to do that?"

"Yes, I can do that, no problem."

"The airfield is dead ahead, I need you to turn left to 270 degrees, then I will turn you to the right and you should have a minute to line up with the runway, which is a very short time but I understand your fuel situation."

"Yes, that's ok, I need to make it short, the fuel gauge has been buzzing and showing zero for five minutes already. Turning to 270 degrees"

"Ok, no need to make any mixture adjustments, just leave everything as they are, we don't want to complicate matters for you. I see you are flying 270 degrees now, well done"

"Understood, no mixture adjustment"

"Now slow your speed to 70 knots, continue on 270 and let your altitude drop as you slow down."

"Slowing to 70 knots on 270, I see my altitude is dropping passing 1500 feet now."

I was now sweating like crazy with nerves and fighting tiredness, I grabbed a quick sip of water.

"I see you visually now, you are doing very well, you are flying very steadily, well done"

"Thank you, please turn me as soon as you can, I felt a slight stutter from the engine I'm going to run out of fuel any second"

"Ok, you need to continue a little longer just to give you time to line up with the runway"

"Yes, I see the runway to my right, continuing on my current course and speed"

"Shortly I will get you to turn right to the runway you will also need to lose speed and lower your flaps, do you know what effect the flaps have and how to lower them?"

"Yes I used them before, I see the flap lever and know how to use it"

"Ok, try now to extend flaps to 10 degrees"

I moved the flap lever with my right hand to the setting required.

"I see your flaps are moving, well done. You will lose some speed, for now, do not allow speed to drop below 60 knots, ok"

"Ok, I can control the speed at 60, I am still descending"

"That's ok, I want you to descend no lower than 500 feet until after the turn, are you happy you can control that?"

"Yes I can control that with the yoke and engine speed, I hope the engine does not stop by using more fuel"

"There is little we can do about that, for now, we need to continue as if you have enough fuel to land. A few seconds more will give you enough time to line up after your turn"

"Ok, understood, I see 2 parallel runways which one is runway 05? Am I aiming for the left or right runway?" Tiredness and stress was fuddling my mind, I should have known which was the left runway.

"We are keeping both clear we will see how you line up after your turn, we would prefer you to land on the left runway as you look at the airfield after your turn, we have emergency vehicles waiting by that runway. Now I need you to apply full flaps, flaps all the way down to 40 degrees please."

"Ok, understood, I think I can manage that I feel in control, flaps 40"

"Well done, but don't get overconfident, keep up your concentration"

"Understood"

"Now begin your turn right to 05 degrees, keep your eye on height, you can allow it to drop to 200 feet keep your speed at 60 until after you complete the turn. Do you see the approach path indicator lights? Do you know what they tell you?"

"Turning right to 05 degrees, speed no lower than 60, descending to no lower than 200. Yes I see the lights I have 3 red and one white"

The path indicator lights help pilots keep height correct, on a correct descent path they should be 2 white and 2 red, 3 red meant I was low, but I didn't want to use the throttle to gain height, I sensed I was at a height that would land me on the tarmac runway, it didn't need to be perfect.

I completed the turn quite quickly, maybe I turned too tight, I ended up on a course between the two runways, I used the rudder to turn left to line up with the runway. I felt another engine shudder as the fuel became more and more starved.

"Good, well done good turn, now allow the plane to descend onto the runway"

"Yes, but I'm a little off line and a little fast I think"

"Ok in a few seconds you can close the throttle allow the plane to descend onto the runway, pull back slightly on the yoke to bring the nose up as you fly over the runway threshold"

"Yes, I'm using the rudder to move left I'm not over the runway, height 100 speed 55"

"Ok you are doing well, you are controlling everything very well, stay calm and allow the plane to land, when you do, close the throttle, apply brakes with your pedals and come to a halt"

I guessed from his angle of view it looked as though I was over the runway, however, I could see I was still 30 feet to the right. More rudder to turn the plane to the runway, I closed the throttle to tick-over and pulled back on the stick. At about 20 feet I was just over the right edge of the runway. I was flying by looking outside, I wasn't looking at any gauges now, it was all visual flying, I felt safer that way.

As I flew over the runway I kicked the rudders right to land in line, just as the plane pointed in the right direction from travelling across the runway to centre, the plane touched down. For all that, I'd say it was a pretty much a perfect landing, no bounce or swerving, more luck than judgement. My shirt soaking wet from sweat, my hands shaking now uncontrollably. I'd done it.

I pressed the brake pedals hard and brought the plane down to 10 knots and took the next right taxiway, even though I had not been instructed to, it just felt better to be off the runway.

"Well done, good landing sir" I could hear applause in the background on the radio

"Thank you, I am glad that is over."

"You may stop where you are. Emergency vehicles are coming to you"

"I request the British Embassy representative to be present, I have diplomatic status, I do not require an ambulance" I lied, I most certainly did need an ambulance, but I was now worried about what the authorities would do with me, I wanted to get to the embassy and nowhere else.

"Stop your engine and wait for assistance" I disobeyed and kept the engine running as an effort to keep people back. I didn't want anyone but the British to get to me. The engine spluttered slightly again, I have no idea what it was running on, the fuel gauges were showing dead empty and the buzzer was really annoying me.

"I am informed Embassy staff are on their way to the airport. Please stop your engine and allow the emergency crews to attend to you"

I saw the blue lights coming for me. I was not going to get out for anyone except Embassy staff. As they approached, I revved the engine and started to move toward an apron parking area in front and to the right. By moving it would keep these vehicles away. I kept moving slowly toward the apron.

"Sir, you may stop where you are and turn off your engine"

"I'm Ok, I will park on the apron and wait in the plane for Embassy staff to arrive" I was probably committing all kinds of offences by ignoring instructions. But I only wanted to deal with Embassy people, after all, I've admitted on the radio I have some kind of secret code, I'm completely compromised now. I was still shaking not knowing how this was going to pan out, but at least I'm safely on the ground.

27. Safe

As I taxied onto the apron next to the runway to a wide parking area, I was surrounded by vehicles. I could not move any further without hitting a vehicle.

"Cessna 172. Sir, please stop your engine and allow us to get you medical attention" came a fairly stern order. I should obey, this will turn out bad if I don't.

"Can you give me information on the arrival of my Embassy representative please" I tried to delay. I decided to part comply and pulled the mixture slider fully out to lean the engine to a stop and turned off all the switches and key switch to bring the aircraft to a full stop. I pulled on the parking brake. It was damned hot sitting in the cockpit in the afternoon sun. People in the vehicles leapt out and approached me. I kept my seat belt on in case they tried to drag me out. The first guy to approach was a policeman. I opened the window. I spoke first.

"Sir, may I request I stay in this aeroplane until my Embassy representatives arrive, I have diplomatic status and respectfully request I am permitted to speak to them first. Another car arrived as the policeman paused for a moment to think how to respond to me. A guy jumped out and approached.

"I am the airport manager, I can tell you a person from your embassy will be here shortly. I am instructed to give you every assistance as a diplomat, would you like to sit in my car and we will drive to somewhere cooler and more comfortable until he arrives?"

"No I will remain here thank you, but I will take some water if you have some" He waved at the policeman to indicate to bring some water. I was starting to feel dizzy with heat and stress. But I didn't want to get out and hand myself over to these people.

"Thank you," I thought I'd start a rapport to help let them know I mean no harm. "I have travelled 6 hours to get here, I hope you excuse my behaviour, but I have important information that is most urgent for my government, I hope you understand why I want to speak to my government before any other authority."

"Of course Sir", the manager replied, I wasn't sure if he was genuine. Yet another car pulled up amongst at least 10 other vehicles of every type that turns out in an airport emergency. A man got out and walked over with a big smile on his face.

"Well done Sir, I am the pilot that spoke to you on the radio, I want to say you made an excellent landing."

"I have 4 hours flying experience before today. Today has tripled my entire flying time, haha" I managed a laugh, the situation seemed to be getting less tense. I think they realised I was important as the Embassy was sending someone without delay. Something that doesn't normally happen with the British.

"Someone from your embassy is coming soon, would you like to come inside where it is cooler?" I would have loved to be somewhere cool, but I felt it safer for my sake to stay where I was

"The Embassy is 40 minutes away, someone will be here very soon don't worry, I understand you have diplomatic status and we will accord you such." I still thought it safer to stay put, with the Russians after me I wasn't trusting anyone.

The small talk continued until finally, I saw a car with diplomatic plates approaching. It came to a halt, and a smartly dressed man got out from the back seat. As he walked up to my window he held out a hand to shake with the manager and the other officials that had gathered around. He turned to me with his hand out, "Madrid, I understand. James Forbes-White British Embassy Angola Attaché, would you care to step over to my car" Of course I could expect nothing less than a double-barrelled name, typical posh Sandhurst accent, but he seemed congenial enough. "I understand you have had an exciting journey today, you look as though you have" With that, I finally unclipped my seatbelt, grabbed my bag and camera and exited the aircraft. The gathered people stepped back to allow me to follow James to his car, I went to shake hands with the controllers that had helped me land safely and thanked them all for their assistance, the handshake turned into more of a finger touch when they saw the state of my bloodied injured hands. Sat in the back with James the car was refreshingly cool.

"We'll get back to the Embassy and you can fill us in on what's been going on"

"After a shower and freshen up, yes" I replied.

"Of course. I'm told you have flown all the way from Lumbala, that's 700 miles away, did you make the entire journey alone, astonishing." We chit chatted the rest of the short journey through the city, I didn't want to say anything until I had spoken to London. I was still shaking, my adrenalin had gone now I needed some good food and water, goodness only knows how bad I must have stunk in that car. Fifteen minutes later we turned into the Embassy compound and I finally felt safe, the feeling overwhelmed me. I have no idea if I fainted or walked, but the next thing I knew I was laying on a bed in a room within the Embassy, in fresh clothes, clean bandages on my hands and obviously washed and clean as much as I could be. As I sat up looking around the room, feeling hungry and very thirsty, I tried to stand up but fell back to sit on the bed. The door opened and a middle-aged lady appeared holding a tray of food and drink. "Good morning Sir, how are you feeling today?"

"Today? What day is it?"

"You arrived here yesterday evening, it's now 11 am. How are your hands, I've done what I can, for now, it looks like clean puncture wounds, but we will get a doctor to look at you shortly, the rest of you looks very bruised, I'm sure you will recover in a few weeks"

"Thank you erm?"

"Elizabeth, I'm on the staff here"

"Thank you Elizabeth, did you dress me"

"Yes, I hope you don't mind, you are not shy are you? I bathed you, cleaned you up and got you into those clothes"

"No that's fine. Thank you for your help" I replied with a slightly bemused tone, wondering how she accomplished lifting my dead weight through all that.

"You're welcome Sir, now have some food and get some rest. I'll tell Mr Forbes-White you are awake." She placed the tray beside me, and left the room, closing the door behind her. I should have been starving but I could only pick at the food but I guzzled the drink down. I ate as much as I could, I don't know why I wasn't hungrier. I was still shaking a lot. The room was more or less bare, just the bed and a couple of non-descript pictures on the walls. I sat for a minute or two, got up and walk gingerly out the door. Elizabeth was walking back down the corridor of the building, I could see out of a window the compound was made up of several buildings inside a walled garden. I asked Elizabeth, "May I sit outside, get my bearings a bit?"

"Yes, the door over there will take you into the garden there are some tables and chairs by the pool, don't wander too far I'm sure someone will be coming to talk to you very soon."

"Thank you Elizabeth. The first and only person I will speak to is in London, is that clear"

"Yes sir, I will pass that message. Please relax and sit by the pool, someone will join you shortly"

I made my way into the garden. It was hot but in the shade, by the pool, it was quite pleasant. The traffic and city noise somewhat spoilt the tranquillity of the garden but it was pleasant enough. I sat at a table with an umbrella for shade just staring at nothing in particular for a few minutes before James came to join me.

"Hello Andy how are you feeling today. Quite a time you've had of it by the looks of it."

"Hi James, yes I'm still very tired and my bruises are hurting a lot, and I am having trouble breathing with this broken rib as it is, I seem to have a nice dent in my rib cage."

"Elizabeth has done all she can, we have sent for a doctor to come to look at you, he will be here very shortly. Andy, you said you are Madrid, we are used to people passing through this office, but we weren't warned you were in country, we have been taken a little by surprise by your arrival."

"Sorry James I have important information for London, I am not speaking to anyone until I have spoken to SIS" I assumed he would know who I was referring to as often an Attaché dealt with National Security and Intelligence matters, indeed quite often they would be an officer of SIS attached to an Embassy.

"I understand, when you are ready, there is a secure line for you. In the meantime, if you need anything, I am here to assist, and Elizabeth can get you food or anything else you need"

"I'll make the call now then, please" I beckoned to indicate for James to lead the way to the telephone. I was taken to an office where there was a desk and phone, James told me to take a seat, he seemed to know the number required without referring to any directory.

"I assume you want Century House, here, it's connected" he spoke into the phone, "Hello, Embassy Angola, I have an urgent call, Madrid will be speaking" He handed me the phone and left the room so I was alone to talk. I wasn't sure how secure the room was, there was always a chance of bugging so I had to be careful. A familiar voice came on the line it was Max, 'C's' assistant, he was on my list of suspected moles.

"Hello Max, I need to speak with 'C' and only with him if I may" I didn't use any name to introduce myself.

"Certainly, one moment". That was easy, it's not usually so simple to get through to the Head of MI6, and clearly, they have word of my arrival in Luanda. The phone clicked, I hoped the line was switching to secret mode. Chris Curwen's voice came on the line.

"Good day to you Andy, I'm told you have got yourself into a little bother"

"Yes just a little" sarcasm was the tone of the moment, "Is this line secure?"

"Yes, you can speak as you wish" Clearly my health was not of immediate concern to 'C', I resented that a little.

"Listen, it is very clear we have a mole, my exact location was known, I was picked up by Russians, they were interested in Gordievsky, he must be in danger, they were trying to find out where he is. I recommend you move him. The thing is, the mole is someone that knew my exact location. It can only be one of the pre-mission team that knows where I was. No question about it, I was in a very remote location, there is no way anyone outside the team involved, would know my location."

"Do you have any suspect? What about UN personnel, was anyone aware you are not Spanish" 'C's' conversation seemed very minimal and out of character.

"No, I don't believe so, nobody here indicated at all they suspected me of being fake. Although I haven't considered the mole can be anyone here, I don't believe that to be so. It can only be one of the UK team"

"UK team being?" Chris Curwen knew the team, he was testing me to see if I had told anyone outside the small team that met in the Reform Club.

"You, Max, Roger and Jean the linguist, no one else for certain"

"Your wife doesn't know where you are?"

"No. She believes I'm on a sailing cruise. I recall you asked me once in London what I thought of Roger, do you have any doubts about his loyalty?"

"Only that the plan he came up with for you was very poor, you knew that but you still took on the risk, a little foolhardy I think"

"If you think that way you should have put a stop to the mission"

"I think we all made mistakes on this one Andy" He made me quite angry, he knew this was a dangerous mission, badly planned, and not enough time allocated.

"Well, for now, You, Max and Roger are top of my list of potential moles," I told him he was on the list of suspects to get back at him for making me angry.

"Ok, Andy, come see me when you get back to London. There's a plane coming for you shortly if you are ok to continue to travel. You are a little emotional about your situation, I hope by the time we meet you have taken time to consider things, I will do the same my side, ok?" He could hear my anger and was trying to calm me down.

"Ok, I'll see you soon in London, I apologise for my short temper I've been put through it a bit here."

"No need to apologise Andy, I understand how you must feel. We will get to the bottom of this very soon." The situation calm again, I hung up the phone. Chris was a nice man for someone in his high position, I liked him and trusted him despite being on my list of suspected moles.

I left the office and found James again. "What's the UN situation James?" I asked because my disappearance would be causing them concern.

"We think it better to let them continue to believe you have gone missing, presumed dead. Unless you have any other plan Andy. We can't let the UN know that we had placed someone inside their ranks. So long as no one from the UN sees you in Luanda we can leave it as it is."

"Yeh, you are probably right, of course. What information is there on my team are they safe?" I had got to know and like the team I was with, all good people in their own way. I hoped they had escaped from Lumbala without incident.

"Information is sketchy, as we are not part of the AVEM, as you know, but I have information they are at Luena, where I understand they have a camp, I believe they will come back to Luanda to make a formal complaint regarding the NPLA. I dare say the UN can't do much about the loss of Comandante Anselmo Gil. The war is bound to have casualties even among the peacekeepers."

"Yes, we left a team with a car at Luena to observe the Cubans there. They can fly to Luanda from that location, that area seemed relatively safe. I wonder about the consequences of the loss of a UN official like you say the UN and the Spanish will make a complaint, and not much will come of it. From our point of view, I think Anselmo Gil's disappearance is quite tidy."

"Yes Andy. I suggest you now relax, a doctor is on his way here, he will see you shortly. You do look a mess"

"I'm hungry now, I'll take some food by the pool I think, see you later I expect." With that I took myself off to the garden, finding Elizabeth on the way, I asked for some food and drink in the garden. I sat for a while thinking about my lucky escape, the epic flight I made, how lucky I was that the rains were late and I wasn't trapped by weather. If I had to avoid any storms during my long flight I'd have run out of fuel for sure. I was lucky to be alive that was for certain, I escaped death how many times in the last few days.

After I ate the food Elizabeth kindly brought me, I sat enjoying the calm of the garden, my head by now used to the noise from the other side of the walls, blocking out the city sounds. I should have found I could start to relax, but I was still shaking. My physical wounds were not too bad, but my mental state, I was sure was not intact.

Soon the doctor arrived to see me. A nice man, his manner very calm, I wasn't sure where he was from, but his accent was English. He gave me a thorough physical examination, as I sat being examined I began to shake more violently. I couldn't understand what was happening. I thought that maybe I had an infection from my hand wounds, but the doctor thought differently. He confessed he was not by any means a psychiatrist, but in his opinion, the events of the last days were causing me to have a mental breakdown, probably post-traumatic stress disorder or PTSD. The stress of my capture and interrogation, being stood in front of a firing squad, my escape, witnessing the killing of Filipe, his wife and Victor. The extreme guilt I was feeling that they should die because they did little more than be civil in a country entirely lacking any civility. The stress of taking a plane and making a six-hour flight with little flying experience. The whole event had an effect on me that I could not get a grip on and control. Clearly, I'm no James Bond with a mental capacity that can take on killing and death so easily. It wasn't a pleasant experience to feel my sanity slipping away. He gave me some pills to calm me down, and a few injections to boost those I had received before leaving England and suggested I should seek help once I return to the UK.

After he left I tried hard to calm myself, the pills the doctor had given me seemed to me to have little effect. I decided I should phone home. I called my father, the only person that knew about my real life.

28. My Dad

Dad and I had developed a code system. We used it every time we met or spoke. A simple code it went something like this when we spoke to each other:-

Hello Andrew, how're things?

Because he used the word Andrew, it meant he was asking about me and my family so I would reply by talking about family things

If he said to me:-

Hello Son how're things?

Because he used the word son it meant he was asking about my work.

To this, I would usually reply, "OK." Quite minimal, I could never tell him the full story

If I added the words, "You know", to this, i.e. "OK, you know"

It meant everything was fine, and what I had done or was doing was something he could read about or see in the media. On those occasions, he would pop out to buy his newspaper, and when he returned, while he was taking off his coat and shoes, I would turn his paper to the relevant article, refold it so it was on top and he could read about what I was up to. He knew he could never discuss it, especially when others were around.

Dad loved this, the idea of having a spy code with a real spy, I was surprised sometimes he didn't cut eye holes in his paper and play the Pink Panther theme music. But Dad knew to be discrete, never to talk, and never to ask. What I asked Dad to do for me was a dreadful thing, I can't imagine the turmoil that at times must have spun in his head. The code system worked for years.

I called Dad at work, his secretary answered the call and put me through to his office. Dad answered with the usual question, Hello son how are things? He used the word son, so he's asking about work.

I replied, "OK, not so good".

This wasn't how the code was supposed to work, failure was never considered an option. Dad knew something was wrong, I could hear from his silence he was wanting to ask but knew he couldn't, if he did, I wouldn't say. I simply said, "I may need some help when I get home". With those few words and the sound of a familiar voice, it became too much for me. I couldn't find a way to speak any words, I somehow stumbled out enough words to tell him I'd be home soon and could he meet me at the airport he'd get details later. I warned him not to be shocked at the way I look. He agreed to whatever I needed and that he wouldn't say anything to anyone at home, really because he didn't know what the story was.

I sat in the pleasant garden of the British Embassy Luanda, I began to think. Someone, and I take some blame in this, caused the deaths of at least three innocent people, and I witnessed it. I take some blame because my presence was so badly planned, within a tiny period of time I had prepared to take on a cover and story that, although had apparently worked, yet in my rush to complete the task in a ridiculous time frame had probably been a contributing factor in those deaths. I did not take time, to consider my movements in Lumbala. I should have planned a better approach. I do think, however, that the UN team, of which I was in charge was in serious danger in that village because Russia was wanting to control and supply the means to counter the UN resolution, but at the time we did not know that. I had suspicions the Cubans were there with a Russian contingent, in an undeclared military camp for subversive activities. If I had not been off on my own in Lumbala, the UN team would probably have retreated and reported the situation for a larger, possibly militarized intervention. The team would have been safe and Filipe Lomba, his wife and colleague would be alive and prospering today. I can only imagine the killing may not have stopped at those three unfortunate people. I can only guess that the entire village may have been slaughtered to prevent the crime from being discovered. No one has been prosecuted for the murders in Lumbala, most probably it has been regarded as an unfortunate consequence of war.

I sat in a comfortable chair in a pleasant garden by a cool swimming pool with orders of food and drink arriving whenever I requested, trying to control my guilt and conscience. I sat thinking why man is such a destructive being, what was the Angolan war about? Greed and power. Why did the British ask me to spy? Greed and power. National Security is rarely about protecting citizens, which is just the story put out into the mass media as the excuse why certain things need to happen. I realised it is all about greed and power. Man is prepared to kill his own race, destroy the land and other creatures we share this planet with. One clever man can persuade other men that his ideal is the perfect solution. Those other men will follow blindly led by their greed and it grows into war.

I was not shocked by the sight of the three murdered bodies, I had seen dead and mutilated human beings many times in my work and even back in time to when I was an eight-year-old boy.

In Maple Cross where I lived as a child before the London orbital motorway M25 was built, was an accident blackspot on the A412. Some idiot architect had decided to make the fast stretch of road from Denham to Maple Cross three lanes! Who had ownership of the middle lane? Clearly, it was uncertain, because there were many fatal accidents. Occasionally I was first on the scene. In those days there were none of the health and safety rules we have today. There were no seatbelt laws, people got involved, rather than stand to video with their mobile phones as they do these days. I witnessed bodies strewn across the road, thrown from their cars many times. I tended to injured people lying in the road until an ambulance arrived for them. I watched people take their last breath. Gruesome, maybe, but I think it made me a better person for the experience. It didn't stop me from throwing up my lunch when I saw what should be inside someone's body, out, but I'm not squeamish of blood and I'm not afraid to get my hands dirty helping someone in a terrible situation. The sight of Filipe and his wife affected me so much because I knew I was partly to blame and killing him was pointless and it began to weigh very heavily on me. The more I thought about it the more I shook in a nervous tension I could not control. Whoever the MI6 mole was, would have to pay for their treachery and I would find the culprit if it was the last thing I did.

The next day a private jet arrived for me at Luanda airport. Before leaving the Embassy I telephoned Karen in London and asked her to inform my Dad when and where I would be arriving, if he would like to be there when I arrive, it was fine by me. I was taken in a diplomatic car bypassing airport security and whisked aboard, avoiding anyone witnessing Comandante Anselmo Gil leaving the country, he was dead too. I had an uneventful flight, in comfort back to England where the plane landed at RAF Northolt, west London.

In the terminal, I was met by my Dad with Karen my secretary, I could see both of them trying to hide the shock of seeing my battered and bruised face. My Dad didn't know what to say, to be honest, he was a little out of his league in the presence of people from SIS. Karen looked shocked and tearful that I was home, we still loved each other despite me being married, and it's hard to explain our relationship. My Dad approached me as I walked into the room, usually, he would shake my hand, I guess he had been warned I had injuries so he, for the first time ever, hugged me. I wanted to hug Karen too but we kept things professional. I could tell she wanted that too, placing herself with her back to everyone she silently mouthed words of care and love to me.

SIS people were present and wanted me to go straight to hospital for a thorough check over. I was to go to Princess Mary's RAF Hospital Halton, at the airfield where I had started to learn to fly a while back and thank God! It was close to my home, my parents also lived in Aylesbury at that time too. Dad, Karen and I were driven in a car by an SIS man, a journey of 35 miles about 40 minutes. We had time for me to give them a short version of what had happened. I didn't say anything about the mole that was hiding somewhere inside MI6. My Dad had a way to calm me down, he always did. He told me that Julie my wife had been told I'd had an accident sailing, something she is quite used to, so it was no big deal for her. She did care, she was a brilliant nurse, serving time at Great Ormond Street Hospital, so I knew I would be in good hands once I got home. At Halton I was checked over by doctors, I was more concerned for my mental health, something had changed inside my head, I could feel it.

As soon as my medical was finished, my dressings changed, Karen took Dad home in the chauffeured car we had travelled from Northolt in, another SIS guy took me home and left me outside with my sailing bag. I went indoors where Julie was busy doing housework. Her first words were typical and I loved that she always took whatever I got up to in her stride, I knew she loved me and knew she would take care of me, though she wouldn't know the real reason for my injuries. Should I have told her the truth? It wasn't the right time - again.

"What have you been up to" she exclaimed as she saw my black eyes and bruises - everywhere.

"I lost my sailing gloves and you know me, Mr Stupid, carried on sailing without and ended the day with really bad rope burns. My hands are a bit stiff and I've lost a lot of skin, but they will mend" I lied to her again. The story wasn't a complete lie, I had once actually done that in a yacht race and my hands had become shredded pieces of meat, so I knew the story fitted.

"Once I couldn't grip the main sheet any longer my hands slipped and I fell onto the cockpit floor cracking a rib, I stood up and got whacked by the boom giving me these lovely black eyes. Quite a funny series of mishaps really"

"You're such an idiot, what am I going to do with you" She replied. Lying to my wife had become second nature and in those days I thought nothing of it, I had done it for so long. But now I felt guilt, nothing but guilt, guilt for everything, for lying, for doing my job badly, for getting people killed.

 Life would not, could not, be the same ever again.

29. Four Days Later

I took a few days off work to stay at home, mostly thinking. I was a changed person, but I couldn't figure out what I wanted to do now. I took the bandages off my hands, the wounds looked good and clean, no sign of infection. They were a little stiff, my right arm was bruised beyond my elbow, it looked as though I had an arm tattoo. I had to get myself motivated again. Julie had been brilliant, what an amazing woman she was, how could I possibly continue to lie to her.

I had recovered enough to return to work to face a major debrief, and it wasn't going to be fun. I went to Century House in London. I wanted to speak to "C" first. My concerns regarding a mole inside the British Intelligence Service were equal to his. Gordievsky was his agent and the threat of assassination was real. We met in his office alone, all bad feelings now gone between us. In my mind, I had eliminated him as a suspect. I reasoned that the mole was now totally exposed, simple detective work would reveal the suspect, he knew that, and, he had ample opportunity to kill Gordievsky should he wish, even if he did not do the dirty work himself. It was a simple matter of finding the common denominator between all those officers and their agents that have disappeared. After some chit chat about my capture and my solo adventure flight from Lumbala to Luanda, we got down to business. If the Americans got word we had another traitor in our midst they would have mistrusted us for a very long time, something we had worked very hard to restore after the embarrassment of the Cambridge Five.

Firstly, we needed to make a list of agents lost under suspicious circumstances or as in the case of Gordievsky, someone had leaked information to the Russians regarding his double-agent activities and subsequent house arrest in Russia. There was no evidence against him, but the tip-off made them suspicious and so, kept him under arrest, as I mentioned earlier in this book.

I didn't know, as I had no access to all the information that Chris had, who would be on the list of the missing. He called his assistant Max and instructed him to compile as quickly as possible the names we needed so we could study and hopefully work out who had something in common with them all. While Max was working on that, we considered the common denominator options. Max had access to all files, but Chris 100% vouched for him that he was not any traitor. There was something in the way he looked at me and I believed him. I had feelings that Roger could be the mole, and there was something about Chris's attitude toward him too that strengthened those feelings. I asked the direct question. "What is it about Roger that you have doubts about?"

"His competence is my concern, he is old school, I have no doubt he can achieve and manage good work, but there is always an air of ineptness about him. The work he did for you was good, he placed you inside the UN very successfully, and he got you the perfect position as leader of the mobile unit that put you where we wanted you to be. It's hard to put my finger on exactly what it is about him, but, as I'm sure you feel the same, there are always parts missing to complete the package, as in your mission. He should have worked with you to get the time in country that you needed for the mission, two weeks was ridiculous."

I took some of the blame for that, "I think I am the problem there. My wife Julie has no idea what I do. It was me that wanted such a small time scale, as my story to Julie could only support a short time away from home."

"But Roger should have instructed you to inform Julie, he should have seen that was the weakest part of the plan, it was his plan and you were acting as his agent on this one."

"I still take the blame for that" I replied.

"Maybe you feel that way, the work you have done here for 17 years has been first class until now, I'd say this mission was a misjudgement, we all make mistakes"

"I don't make mistakes in matters like this, and as a consequence of my misjudgement people have died" I tried to assert my feelings on the matter, though not defending Roger at all.

"Roger should have helped you put Julie into the picture, it would have worked"

"I should have told Julie before we married. I didn't because one failed relationship made me worry I'd lose her too."

"You should have spoken to Colin Figures he would have advised you on that if those were your concerns" Colin Figures was the Head of MI6 in 1982 when I met Julie. His reputation as an unstuffy, approachable conciliator, should have made him quite amenable to helping me with my personal problems.

"I tell you what" Chris continued. I have another meeting, we can't do much until Max produces a list of those agents for us. Let's take a break and reconvene here in two hours."

"Sure no problem" With that he hurriedly left the room a busy man indeed.

There wasn't much I could do, so I left the room and went down to my office. I spoke to Karen, asked how she was and chit chatted for a few minutes. She was always beautiful, and very good, if not the best at her job. I was so lucky she worked with me. She showed real concern for my health, she could see that I was not mentally fit either. She reassured me that if ever I needed to talk she was available 24/7. I knew that anyway. I'd have loved to have the excuse to go to her home and be with her for a while, she had such a calming lovely manner, but, I was married, it wasn't appropriate. After chatting to Karen, I decided to kill some time by visiting my favourite place, the gun range, maybe I could loose off some frustration.

Downstairs in the range, I signed in, Pete was behind the desk, a real pro, he knew his stuff, ex-military, probably special services, I never asked, just assumed, he was highly professional. "Jeez, you've been in the wars Sir" he exclaimed in his northern accent.

"Yes, quite literally" I wasn't going to talk about it, and he knew not to press further.

"I have something new for you, you'll like this Sir. Glock have just produced a new gun, the 19. Should suit you being a lefty" meaning I was left-handed.

"Let's see it then, what's so special about it"

"Easy to use and break down and for you, a lefty, no awkward safety lever to mess around with. Light, easy to conceal, There's a double trigger, see." He showed me the weapon, pulling back the slide to double-check and show me the chamber was empty before handing it to me, I liked it. It fitted nicely in my hand. There was a different trigger, a kind of double mechanism, the first part acting as a kind of safety mechanism to prevent accidental discharge, and the trigger weight was nice. Being a great shot with my left hand, it was always less efficient having to use both hands on the weapon to click off the safety lever. A right-handed person can use their thumb, a lefty has to find a way to use both hands to grip, to use the thumb with the right hand. Not ideal, and I was useless shooting right-handed.

"There are 6 magazine sizes. It's just out, you are the first to see it"

"I want it already, can I have one?"

"I already got you one, I knew you'd like it"

He went through everything about the gun, how to break it down for checking and cleaning, how to drop the magazine, for this, he showed me a few different methods, one-handed and two, so that the magazine drops into your hand or the floor. He could change magazines in two seconds in one easy move by using an index finger grip on the magazine. I practised a few times and got it down to three. I liked this gun a lot and I was going to be the first to have one. I took the gun to a firing station and prepared and fired all fifteen rounds. For a first-time firing, I did great, I got thirteen on target in the head and body. With some practice, I'd get them all in. After an hour, Pete produced a box containing my new gun. We went through all the parts, cleaned and prepared it for use. I went back to the station and fired a magazine off. I loved it. I told him I'd take it now to practice at a range near my home, not normal practice but sometimes that happened. Officers weren't usually expected to carry or use weapons but we were all trained in their use. He gave me a lockable case to take it away. I signed and thanked him for it and said I'd be back to practice often. I like the gun range it's a fun sport in my opinion.

I re-joined "C" in his office to continue the meeting. Max had completed a list of names for us. The three of us went through it to try to find the common link between them all. I was on the list, though not killed, I was supposed to have been, a little alarming to see your name on a list of killed officers and agents. On the list were agents I knew too. Looking at the dates, we could not place Roger on the suspect list as he wasn't even working for SIS when some of them were compromised. Maybe it was down to one traitor, maybe there were several, again. Roger could certainly be on a list if there were more than one mole, but he could not be responsible for all our lost colleagues. We could not find any link, it was odd, the mole was clever. I decided to go talk with Roger. 'C' said he would come too, but had a little business to take care of first and would meet at Roger's office in ten minutes. I went down to my office, took my new Glock from its box and stuffed it down the back of my trousers. I don't know why I did that. Maybe, I felt if we needed to arrest Roger there could be trouble, it was just an instinctive feeling, and I usually trusted my instincts.

I went to Roger's office, his secretary buzzed him and I was told to go through straight away, just as 'C' joined me in the office. We entered Roger's office together, of course, he was shocked to see my battered face. "Wow, Andy you've been through it, sorry."

"Why are you sorry, it goes with the job sometimes?" I said in a suspicious tone. We sat on his sofa and began to talk through what had gone wrong. The gun down the back of my trousers was quite uncomfortable. He knew what had happened to me, but it was a way to break the ice to gently interrogate him without him realising. Chris was a superb interrogator, I don't think Roger even realised what we were doing. It became clear to me he was either very good at covering his tracks or he was innocent. For me, it was slightly disappointing, as my opinion of him was so bad that I just wanted him to be the baddie, but I was smart enough to know I had to be fair and do this properly. After many questions, Chris asked him directly, if anyone outside of the four of us, namely, me, Chris Curwen, Roger and Max had, while I was in Angola, asked about me, and where I was. It was the bluntest question. The question was straight forward and Roger realised then he was being interrogated. He thought for a moment, "Well, one person outside the four you mention but was part of your preparation team, Jean, she did pop in occasionally to ask how you were doing, how was your Spanish standing up, and general stuff like that"

I asked "Roger, did you tell her where I was"

"No, never" Roger declared innocently

"Could she have found out by looking at your files?"

"Not as far as I know, but she is quite friendly with Kate my secretary"

I asked 'C' if he knew how long Jean had been in service with SIS. He did not know, he called Max by phone and asked him to find out. Ten years was the answer. She has been in service over the entire period that all those listed agents have been disappearing. Kate overhearing our conversation appeared in Roger's doorway. "Sorry to interrupt Sir, I see Jean often in the mess hall and sometimes she comes here when passing to say hi. She may have seen files on my desk". I sat for a moment and thought about this. Why was she passing by? Suddenly it all added up, I sprung up out of the seat and ran out of the office. I ran down the corridor, I could hear 'C' shouting after me. I flew down the stairs not waiting for a lift to arrive and ran into the translator's room. A large room with many of the SIS translators sitting at desks transcribing documents from or into whatever language was required. Jean was sitting at a desk at the back of the room. I walked fast across to her, she saw me coming, I knew instantly from the look on her face she was shocked to see me. I was supposed to be dead, she hadn't heard I was alive. "Sir, Andy, I ...." Without a word, I pulled the gun out from the back of my trousers under my jacket and fired three shots, one into her head and two in her body as she recoiled backwards from the impact of the first bullet hitting dead-centre of her forehead. She was dead before she hit the floor. Everyone in the room went into panic mode, just as 'C' and Roger ran into the room. Women and men screaming, some jumping up and running out of the room, some ducking under their desks. They didn't know I was only after Jean. I heard some crying. I dropped my new and now used Glock 19 onto the desk and put my hands up to indicate there would be no more shooting. "Andy! What have you done? Why? We could have arrested her, maybe found out who she was passing messages to" 'C' shouted at me.

I hadn't planned to react this way, I just did it in a rage, I lost control, completely out of character, and I'd lost it. I felt nothing for Jean only rage. She had been responsible for the deaths of many, the pain of the losses for their families, the danger to British security, my pain and near-death experience. There was no doubt in my mind. I did not care if I was wrong at that moment, I knew she was guilty of treason. In 1989 treason was still punishable by death, and she was dead.

I stood with my hands up as security men arrived guns drawn. 'C' stood them down. He spoke out loud to everyone present. "The situation here has not happened. No one is to speak of it to anyone. We have this under control now. Is that clear?" Some people through their tears replied "Yes sir", the rest remained silent. 'C' took control, and ordered the security team to take care of the staff in the room, anyone requiring assistance could see the doctor, but was quite clear that not a word was to be spoken about this. I started to shake again, quite violently, I didn't want to, but I could not control it. I took one look at Jean, parts of her brain splattered against the wall behind, the look of shock still on her face. I threw up onto the floor next to her. I always do when I see people's insides, out.

Chris and Roger put their arms around me, and led me out of the room, a security guy took my gun from the table. I held my head down in shame of what I had just done. We went up to my office. Chris asked, "What on earth has convinced you she was the mole?"

I answered calmly "Jean was the only person involved in my preparation for this mission NOT present at our final meeting before I left for Angola. If she had seen the mission statement I wrote, she would have known it was my direct intention to be exposed as a British spy and dangled as bait. If she knew that, she would have never risked passing any information"

30. Aftermath

Guided to my office by Chris and Roger, I sat on a sofa in my office. Karen came in from her room, she could see all was not well. She probably hadn't heard the gunshots from several floors above the linguist's room. She had no idea what had just happened. Chris spoke to her "Look after Andy, do not leave him alone, do not let him out of your sight"

"Why? What's happened? She could see the stress and look of horror on my face, she knew something bad had happened.

"There's been an event downstairs, I need to go and sort things out, I'll be back shortly. Take good care of him." He left my office, in a hurry to get downstairs and get the mess sorted out. He didn't want this to get out into the public domain for sure, he had to speak to all those witnesses and to organise a "clean-up". Roger went with him, leaving Karen and me alone.

"Andy, what's happened? Can you tell me, you look awful" She sat next to me and held my hand by my fingers so as not to hurt my palms" She was so gentle, and as always amazingly pretty.

"I've messed up. I'm probably going to be arrested. Shit! I've messed up big time. This is the end of my career here." I said quite calmly but shaking quite violently, I was having a complete breakdown now. Am I supposed to know I'm cracking up, is this one of those catch 22 situations? If I know I'm going mad, I can't be mad?

"Tell me Andy. What has happened?" I didn't want to tell her the dreadful way I just behaved, telling Karen I'd lost it was admitting to her I'd failed and failed, totally.

"Jean, it was Jean the linguist, do you know her?" I said not looking at Karen but into the space of the room.

"What about Jean?"

"I worked it out, she was the mole in MI6, it was her that caused, how many people to die or suffer, how many? I just shot her dead"

"You killed her!" despite this news Karen didn't let go of my hand or gave any indication that she was repulsed by my action.

"She was the one that was passing information on officers and agents here in SIS. Her treachery, *she*, has cost the lives of how many?" I'm more thinking aloud than informing Karen of the events of the last few minutes.

"Jean! Oh God, what have I done?" Karen exclaimed as she put her hands on her head.

"What do you mean? What have you done?" I looked at Karen, how could she be part of this?

"While you were in Angola, she came to see me a few times. She asked how you were doing, how was your Spanish."

"And you told her what?" I looked at Karen now realising she could be part of this too.

"I thought she was secure, she was part of your prep team. I didn't see the harm."

"You told her where I was?"

I had been sending data burst messages from a long-range transmitter, it sent messages in a quick burst of data to eliminate the risk of detection. Messages received were passed, after assessment, to Karen for her to transcribe a copy for my records and to those that needed to know. Karen knew where I was every day.

"I could have. Oh my God, what have I done!" she repeated. "A couple of times she came in here as she was passing. She seemed very nice, and I… I told her you had found a Russian camp in Lumbala. Oh my God I have been so stupid"

"Firstly, why would she be passing here, her office is several floors down? Even though she was part of my preparation team, she had no right to that information. Jeeezus Karen!"

"She seemed so nice and she seemed so concerned about you........" Karen realised what a huge mistake she had made. I could feel a rage rising again, but this time I kept control, I couldn't hurt this beautiful girl.

I put my head in my hands, "Karen, oh Karen"

"I will have to resign" She now fully understood the mistake she had made, on the Angola job everyone has made huge mistakes, she wasn't alone in the blame, all of us involved were.

"That will be up to 'C'. He may have to charge you, I don't know. I don't know what will happen after this, it's all up to him now. Karen we've all made big mistakes with this, I don't know how we've all got it so wrong." She began to cry, she realised her career was over too.

I could see she was genuinely upset, I tried to calm her. "Would you like a cup of tea?"

"I'll make it," She said, our hands slowly slid apart as she got up. She walked to her office blowing her nose as she walked. She brought a pot of tea back to the sofa and we sat, drinking tea not saying much, there wasn't anything to say until we both knew our futures.

After a few minutes 'C' returned. "Ok, I've organised a clean-up, all staff have been ordered under no circumstance to speak of this outside this building. A team are on their way to Jean's house to see if they can find any evidence."

"Sir," Karen began bravely and composed, "I have to confess to a part in this" She explained how Jean had visited, it was virtually all we needed as proof Jean was a mole. Hard physical evidence would provide that, if necessary, would prove the linguist's guilt in court - if it ever came to that. "I'm not letting this get out. We took years to convince the Americans we are to be trusted and leak-free, it will ruin years of work if this gets to them."

"They probably already know" I interjected ironically, "there are probably more moles in this leaky building"

"I hope for the sake of the country they never know" 'C' finished, "You two go home, take few days off. I'll call when I need to speak to you." With that he left, lots to do. I believe he knew he had also messed up too, allowing the Angola mission to go ahead. It was a poor plan, he should have stopped it. There was a plus side to this at that moment. Without this major cock-up, the mole may never have been revealed, we all understood that. More lives have probably been saved by this monumental cock-up.

Karen and I cleared the tea, she offered to take me home, "My car is at Amersham station, I can catch a train it's ok" I misunderstood her offer. "No, come home with me, I don't want to be alone and you shouldn't be alone either. Come to mine with me please."

"Well, erm, ok" I was happily married, I hadn't been alone outside Century House with Karen since my marriage. But it was clear to me that neither of us was in the frame of mind to do anything inappropriate, difficult as that always is. I made a call to Julie at home explaining I had a lot of work to catch up on after being off work for so long. As always, the lie was easy, but now I did feel a lot of guilt. We called 'C's' office and informed his secretary where we were going.

We made the short journey to Karen's home without a word being spoken to each other. We were both concerned now for our future. It seemed to me that 'C's' cover-up activities meant there hopefully wasn't going to be any arrests for murder or manslaughter today. He was interfering with that evidence, which also meant he believed that Jean was the mole. At this stage, I don't know what it was that convinced him of that. For sure he was worried there may be a negative reaction to this if the Americans found out. One thing for sure they wouldn't find out from me, I never trusted them anyway.

Arriving at Karen's apartment she told me her lodger no longer stayed there so we were alone and free to talk openly. It was some years since I last went there, our annual after office party fling had finished when I met Janine and then Julie. Karen made more tea and plated some snacks, we sat on her soft sofa at either end, not touching each other. "I'm going to quit," I said, "If I'm not in trouble if 'C' does a cover-up, I can't stay that's obvious. I've been compromised, I can't hold my head up in Century House any longer, I can't stay."

"Me too, I've made a whopper of an error talking to Jean and I nearly got you killed. I can't live with that" I knew Karen would find work elsewhere, no problem at all, she was that good, and probably would find better-paid work too.

"Well, there is no need for you to worry about what nearly happened to me" I emphasised 'nearly' I tried to reassure her, but I knew it wouldn't affect her thinking. "It's my job, I always know the risks. Please don't worry about what happened to me. I'm so sorry it has to end this way". In my head there was a constant video running, I kept seeing Filipe, his wife and Victor laying in pools of blood in odd twisted positions, I kept getting the vision of Jean's face as it recoiled back from my perfect shot to her head, her brain splattering on the wall behind. The video wouldn't stop.

I didn't know what would happen next, would someone be coming to arrest me or both of us, was my future the inside of a prison cell? Now and then I'd start shaking, violently, my head felt as though it was fizzing, something inside my head had blown a fuse and was now sparking and arcing. We could do little for each other, other than reassure ourselves we'd get through it all somehow, sip tea and nibble a few snacks for hours, until late at night Karen got up to go to bed, I'd never seen her look so shattered. She told me I was welcome to stay and there was a place next to her. I couldn't, I'm married and this was just not the time. I spent the night sitting on her sofa, drinking tea and watching TV to distract my mind after she left for bed. I did once or twice throughout the night look in on her to make sure she was ok and not crying alone. She was sleeping and looked so beautiful, I left her to sleep. It would have been so much better to have laid down next to her put my arms around her perfect body. The comfort she could give me would have been so perfect.

In the morning I was stood at the lounge window looking out at the world outside, people were busy going wherever, I was just staring, in a dream-like state, a million issues going through my mind trying to shake out the pictures and scene of Filipe and Jean. I'd witnessed the murder and I'm guilty of it. Sipping yet another cup of tea the world outside was blissfully unaware of yesterday's dreadful events, the busy people outside, contributing to the country's wealth, paying their taxes - mostly. What's it all about? Karen walked into the room from her bedroom. "Morning Andy" she looked stunning in her pyjamas, girlie, sexy, hair in a mess, her breasts jiggling as she walked toward me. She put an arm around my waist and rested her head on my shoulder and we both stood for a minute looking out of the window. "You look beautiful even with no makeup," I spoke without even looking at her. "What shall we do today?" she asked not looking at me either, both of us just staring out the window in a dreamlike state. "Two things." I replied "One we should go to Century House and hand in our resignations to 'C' if you still feel you want to do that. Two we need to decide where we are going. Can we be together?"

"You'd leave Julie for me?"

"Yes, in a moment"

"I can't allow that"

"Why not" I now turn to look at her "We've kind of been together longer than Julie and I"

"You have a gorgeous daughter and one on the way, I can't allow you to leave them with no father"

"All of a sudden you are full of morals?"

"If it were just Julie, I'd fight her for you, I love you more than you can imagine, but your children, no, I can't do that. My parents divorced when I was 8, I know how that feels, I couldn't do that to your family" I went into silent mode trying to figure a way to be with Karen. I knew she was seven years older than me, but this woman was everything I could dream of, perfect in every way, even under these circumstances she was keeping calm, moved in a balanced controlled way, like you see athletes move, somehow they always look in control of gravity.

"So where are we, how can we move on?" Had Karen thought about us, did she have a plan?

"Right now I can't think about that. We should go write our letters of resignation and hand them in personally. Do you think we will be permitted to enter Century House?"

"Only one way to find out". I looked a mess, I went to shower, while Karen made her coffee. I had no clean fresh clothes or even a toothbrush, so I brushed my teeth with my finger, the toothpaste providing some kind of mouth freshness from a night of drinking tea. I found a razor in her bathroom cabinet, a Ladyshave type, I didn't care where or what it had been used for, I needed to shave, my facial hair grows so fast, it did a reasonable job if a little painful on my bruises. She came into the bathroom for her shower as I was drying up. We were just like a couple, natural together in our nakedness, not shy. I loved being with her, I wanted to be with her so much. I dressed and left the bathroom and sat watching the morning news on TV. Nothing about a killing, nothing about a body found in the Thames, good.

We caught a train back to Lambeth North Station and walked into the entrance of Century House, not sure what the reaction would be by anyone inside. At the security check table we were both frisked more thoroughly than usual, but passed through without incident, although I did notice the security guard telephone someone after we left the desk. A few heads turned to sneak a look at us both and I definitely felt uneasy. We went up in the lift to our office, alone in the lift we both said how people were looking, I suppose it's only natural I would have done the same. Once in our office, Karen sat at her desk to write our resignations. She was very efficient at her work, ten minutes later a letter for each of us was ready to be signed. She called up to 'C's' office and asked for an appointment to go see him, surprisingly we were told we could go immediately.

We sat at Chris's desk, a first for me I had always sat on his sofa, so I guessed he knew this was a formal meeting. Without talking too much, apart from his enquiry as to how I was feeling and how my injuries were, we passed him our letters. He read mine first and placed it on his desk. He then read Karen's and dropped it straight into the bin "Refused" he said to her "I'm not letting you go, you are too good at your job, I want you to reconsider."

He looked at me "I also want you to reconsider, I'm not going to bin this letter. You are not the only person to blame for the debacle that has happen, the work you have done since you joined SIS has been first class. No one knows how you obtained so much information on so many businesses and people, no one seems to know, it was brilliant work." I looked at Karen and she gave me a little nod indicating I should tell him. I told him the Xerox story in full. "Have you ever serviced my photocopier?" He said half-joking, half in fear.

"I could hardly walk in here and pose as a service engineer, I think someone would have noticed who I am" "But we should think about a method to delete the drives automatically"

"Yes, the technical department can easily build a device to do that, for them it will be quite simple. They can look at my device add a new part to make it a permanent fitting inside each machine"

"Can you do that for me, get every machine in the building protected"

"Of course"

"Andy I want you to consider staying with us, we don't like letting people go, you have a job here if you want to stay"

"I'll consider it if the doctors and HR can assess me, I feel something inside has been changed by events I've experienced. I know I should be tougher, I want to be tougher, but my head is fizzing" It was the only way I could describe how I felt.

"Ok, get yourself checked over fully, full mental assessment" I wanted this, I knew something was not right in my head.

Karen spoke, "Do you want me to continue to work with Andy?"

"Well, I think it best to separate you two love birds" Damn! How did he know, we were always so careful not to do anything at work to show we were in a relationship of some kind, and I wasn't sure at that moment what that was. "But, if Andy stays, I will give you the choice, you can work anywhere. I'd prefer you didn't stay together, it's not a safe situation you put yourselves in, there are security issues, do you not see that? Andy is married, it could place you in danger of blackmail. God knows, there are even some in this building that would blackmail you. I could order you both to split, but I will be discrete on the matter, for now, you've been through a lot and I don't think it will do either of you any good to add to the pressures you are both under right now." How on earth did he know we were an item, I guess there are spies everywhere. He was being too soft on us, in retrospect, he should have ordered us to part, it was the right thing to do. But, at least it wasn't a gay relationship that a few personnel in Century House were indulging in, that would be far more dangerous from a security point of view, at least in those days it was.

We agreed I would get myself assessed and Karen would reconsider and give him an answer very soon. Things needed to settle down and become normal again, if there is such a thing in MI6. My resignation has not been accepted formerly or denied to this day.

31. My Brain Is Broken

After the meeting with 'C', Karen returned home, and I went to HR to arrange a full assessment of my health. I was put through a similar test on a computer to the recruiting test I had taken so many years ago. I'd been working at SIS for seventeen years by now. I failed miserably. I couldn't remember a lot of things that I should either. I was sent to a psychiatrist. In that meeting a very bizarre thing happened, I sat in the room on a sofa, a cliché situation if ever there was one. The doctor started to talk to me and I chatted away in Spanish, totally unaware I was doing so. "Andy, can you stop and start again, I do not speak Spanish" I stopped speaking and thought about it, I couldn't work out what he was saying I had no idea I was speaking the wrong language, and I couldn't figure which language I was supposed to speak. "Can you talk to me in English please" Ah now I knew, I talked in English for the rest of the session. At the end of my time with the psychiatrist, he wrote a letter to 'C'. I didn't read what the letter contained but I guessed it wasn't good. The results of all the tests were sent to MI6, and I was told verbally that although my physical injuries were minor, I knew that, I could feel my body recovering, but, mentally I had suffered a complete breakdown, causing multiple types of amnesia. I guessed myself I was suffering a breakdown, certain thoughts or action caused me to start shaking and sweating. I was nervous, shy, and unable to do my work!

My multiple amnesia is a problem and I put it all down to the events in Angola. The stress and physical multiple beatings were the cause. With time I have recovered most memories, the amnesia that remains is odd, I cannot recall or learn anything that may offer me the chance to return to SIS work. For instance, I cannot learn or speak languages. Later in life, in the next part of my story, I went to college, evening classes, to re-learn Spanish, as it was a dream of mine to live, or at least to have a holiday home in Spain. I struggled to learn, I achieved an 'O' level Spanish, and eventually overt time and many hours struggling, I could hold a conversation again.

Simply put my broken brain prevents me from doing what it thinks to be anything dangerous, and reacts to SIS, MI6 and MI5 (I will discover this later). It's not a conscious thing, it does it by itself. Even something mildly dangerous, such as climbing the mast of a yacht will bring on some form of reaction, I can ignore it or overcome it, that is my new challenge in life. Writing this book and recalling the story, some memories cause me to become emotional. You could say that is normal given the events I went through, but, add to that, odd things happening, such as words being spelt completely backwards, or, spelt in capital letters, subconsciously I am shouting out the words. I find it quite interesting.

Here's what the doctors told me, in short:

Retrograde amnesia is the inability to recall memories before the onset of amnesia. One may be able to encode new memories after the incident. People suffering from retrograde amnesia are more likely to remember general knowledge rather than specifics. Retrograde amnesia is usually temporary and can be treated by exposing them to memories from the loss. (Later in my story, I begin to tell people who I was, it helped me tremendously with this form of amnesia)

Post-traumatic amnesia is generally due to a head injury, for example: a fall, a knock on the head or in my case, a damn good kicking.

Dissociative amnesia results from a psychological cause as opposed to direct damage to the brain caused by head injury, which is known as organic amnesia. Dissociative amnesia can include:

Repressed memory the inability to recall information, usually about stressful or traumatic events in a person's life, such as a violent attack or disaster. The memory is stored in long-term memory, but access to it is impaired because of psychological defence mechanisms. Persons retain the capacity to learn new information and there may be some later partial or complete recovery of memory. (I found this to be true once I start to tell my story)

Dissociative fugue is also known as fugue state. It is caused by psychological trauma and is usually temporary and unresolved, and therefore may return. An individual with dissociative fugue disorder is unaware or confused about his or her identity and will travel in journeys away from familiar surroundings to discover or create new identities. It is extremely rare.

Source amnesia is the inability to remember where, when or how previously learnt information has been acquired while retaining the factual knowledge.

Situation-specific amnesia can arise in a variety of circumstances resulting in Post-Traumatic Stress Disorder or PTSD.

Semantic amnesia affects semantic memory and primarily expresses itself in the form of problems with language use and acquisition.

It's quite a list!

I returned home after a day of tests, medicals and assessments of every kind, a thorough job had been done on me. I didn't object, it was what I wanted and needed. I was quite exhausted by it all though. I think I slept for twelve hours. The next phase of my life was pure turmoil, I have no idea how Julie put up with me, she seemed to be such a strong, understanding lady, yet still, had no idea what I was, did or had suffered.

I talked with Julie, I had every intention of telling her the truth finally. But, I just couldn't I knew she would never believe me, the story was too incredible. We sat together that evening. I told her that I couldn't do my job any more, I didn't say which job. I wanted to do something different, move away and start again. She listened, seemed to understand and agreed that whatever I wanted to do if I showed her it was a good plan for our future and would be safe and secure for our children she would support me fully. How many wives would be like that? She was such a great woman. I spoke nothing of my life in SIS to her, I spoke only about the printing job. I was such a coward.

I decided to speak to my Dad. The next day I went to Maple Cross where the printing works now occupied a large factory space, it had grown quite well and was one of the busiest printers in the area. I sat in my Dad's office, he started to speak first, he had news for me. He was planning to retire. If I wanted the company I could have it. The catch was, I had to buy it. He had had the company valued, I was given first refusal to buy it. I couldn't believe it. There was no way I could afford to pay the price he was asking. On the one hand, this was the kick in the backside I needed to spur me into moving away, on the other hand, this felt so terrible. Even though I had worked in SIS, I had still put in the hours at my second job at the printing company. He had always said I should work at the printing company for a lower wage, as one day the company would be mine, and working cheaply was my investment in my future. I felt betrayed, he was asking me to buy it. I had mixed and muddled feelings, with everything else going on I could not cope with this extra burden. I could not afford to buy the company at the price he was offering me, it was another straw, and it was probably the final one, and it broke my back let alone the camels. He couldn't have given me this news at a worse time. But he thought he was helping me to break away from SIS, it was his way of saying I had done enough in that job, time to be normal. I didn't stay to talk about my problems at SIS, I thought it best to go home before our chat turned into a blazing row. It did in a way, but only in my head.

At home, I told Julie the news. She was flabbergasted, how could my father treat me this way! I had mixed feelings, I didn't have the right to own the business, but I was always led to believe I would inherit it. I'm not a greedy person, but for some reason this hurt deeply. As there was no way we could afford to buy the printing business, it had grown so well, we decided together that evening to move away, start a new life. Of course, she still didn't know the full reason why we should move on, but now I had yet another reason not to tell her what was about to become my past, and the reason was, I wasn't in that life any longer.

32. A New Life In Devon

Julie and I started to think about what I should do. We decided as I liked sailing and boats of every kind, we should look to do something in the marine industry. In those days there was still no web sites for information that we have today. The only way we could look for something was the Exchange and Mart, business section. We knew I wanted to work for myself, I didn't want to work for anyone ever again. The only form of business for sale in that line was mostly chandlers' shops and boat storage. I wasn't keen, it was obvious the reason for those companies were for sale as they could not sustain enough income to survive. It became apparent that this type of business survived only by the continuous turnover of new owners putting money into the business until it went broke. The old owners would sell to a new dream maker and repeat. I knew I didn't want a shop, all one could do was turn up in the morning, open the door and hope someone would walk in and buy something. There was little one could do to improve or make it different to how all the previous owners had run the business. We were looking to live anywhere, anywhere at all.

Finally, we found something different, for sale was a small business in Torquay, Devon, England. A little company manufacturing buoyancy aids, a similar product to life jackets. This sounded more exciting. A company like this could be developed, promoted, made more efficient, all the challenges I wanted. The reason for the sale seemed genuine, the owner wanted to retire. I made enquiries and within a few days, we were off to Torquay to go look.

Downsouth (Torquay) Ltd was a small business in Wellswood, Torquay. In a 3500 square foot factory space down a tiny lane (which was a bit of a problem, as large vehicles had difficult access). The owner, his wife and a few staff worked making one style of buoyancy aid, in six sizes. It all seemed to work well. The only drawback was, that the lease on the factory only had eight years left. I considered that if I could make a success of this, it wouldn't be a problem to renew the lease or move to a better location. The printing company had moved several times, I knew what was involved in that. The accounts and books looked ok, nothing special, but I believed with some work I could build the business. It seemed ideal. There was one huge drawback, the owner only invoiced his customers once a year, unbelievable! This was something I'd have to address quite quickly. He had a good list of customers, from shops and chandlers to boat hire companies on the Norfolk Broads. The selling price was affordable for me. It seemed just what we were looking for, and, as a bonus, it was located in a beautiful town on the coast in Devon, South West England, a perfect place to bring up our children. We had to make this happen. We returned to our home in Aylesbury feeling quite excited about it and during the journey home decided of all the businesses we had looked at, this one seemed to fit the bill.

The first problem, raising the money. We hadn't thought too hard about money, simply because we didn't know what we would find and the price that would be. To purchase 'Downsouth' we would need to sell our house, buy a house in Devon, and buy the company.

Have you ever tried buying a house and know the difficulty and stress that brings? Try buying a business as well, and coordinate the two so that you can move into your new home, learn a new trade, run a new business, and not make a complete hash of it all, while bringing up a child, with one on its way, 200 miles away from the nearest family or friend to help, in a town you've never been to before!

We did the deal with the owner, settled on a price for the business, plus stock at the time of completion. It was going to be ours. First thing on the list of things to do, get money. We put our house on the market, if it sold as priced we would make a good profit, as house prices were rocketing at that time, it could not be better. Houses in Devon were far cheaper to buy, so there would be money left over to put into the pot for the business purchase. We still needed more. A relative of Julie had sold his greenhouse nursery property in Watford, he offered us £30,000 no interest, he was old and didn't need the money for himself, so we accepted his kind help. In those days banks were throwing money at people, for me, it was even easier. I called Karen, without Julie knowing. I remembered her father was in banking, maybe she could ask him to help. Without any interview or paperwork, I got more than I needed at a very good low-interest rate. After everything was completed I even had over £30,000 too much, which helped a lot.

Six months later, our house was sold, a house in Torquay was purchased, the contract signed for the business in Torquay. We agreed the contract would be completed three months after moving to Torquay. I would use those three months at the company learning how to make buoyancy aids. Everything fell into place perfectly, we could not believe our luck, but I don't recommend doing if you have a faint heart.

The day of the move arrived. Our journey to Devon took forever. Joanne our first daughter, wanted a hundred toilet breaks, and if I got a pound for every time she said "Are we there yet" I would not have needed any loan at all. It took us six hours, a journey that should have taken three. Arriving in Torquay the removal lorry had been waiting for hours for us. Fed up with waiting the men had broken into our house, moved all our stuff in and they were just finishing up. They explained they had no trouble getting through the bathroom window easily, which was an extension from the house into the garden at ground floor level. The first job, as soon as possible, would be to organise the manufacture of metal bars for the window to make the house secure. Though we didn't know it at the time the house would become a money pit. It's a story on its own that house. If it wasn't such hard work it would be hilarious.

33. House Of Horrors

I want to tell you the story of our house in Ellacombe, Torquay in one chapter, I could probably write a book on the saga of the house alone, so this is the short version. It's not really relevant to the storyline of MI6, but it contributed to the stress I was under. Remember, we do all this while learning a new business and bringing up two children. Our second daughter Lynne was born at Torbay Hospital shortly after moving to Devon. I don't think that makes her Devonian, but she does have the laid back, relaxed attitude that people in Devon have, there must be something in the water here.

It was no easy task to bring up two children in a town where we know no one and have no friends to babysit. The print company business didn't sell, in the end, my father just closed it down and my parents had moved to Malvern, Worcestershire. Supposedly, as we were told by them, this was so that they were roughly in the centre of a triangle from all three of their sons, they claimed they could visit each of us easily and equally. It wasn't true, we are at least double the distance, which, kind of showed Julie and me where we stood in their life. Moving to Malvern was only about living in a nice place, and that is fine, but don't tell me it was to be equidistant from us all. They visited my brothers, and my mum babysat for them often, but for us, never. She claimed we were too far away! We fell out big time over this issue, in addition to the printing company problem, I didn't speak to them for years. When we did get back to speaking terms they claimed they never asked me to buy the company. I think in their minds they had realised maybe they had made a mistake and had blocked it from their memory in their old age. I know the printing business matter to be true because, one, Julie remembers, even if my head is playing games, and two, it was the spur that kicked us on to moving away from Buckinghamshire to Devon.

So, back to our house. It was a 150-year-old, four-bedroom, almost a semi-detached, I say almost, where it connected to what was a chip shop next door at ground level, was an alleyway, but our house had a 'flying attachment' as the surveyor put it. Basically, one of the bedrooms on the first floor was the bridge over the alleyway. I found it's a great way to introduce myself to people when they asked where I live, I would say, "I have a house in Ellacombe, and I've almost got a semi". A lounge, kitchen diner, connecting via a tiny lobby to a bathroom which was an extension into a courtyard walled garden. There was no front garden, the front door opened directly onto the street. The garden was to the side. The back of the house, because Devon is quite hilly, was at ground floor level completely underground, so there were no windows at all. Upstairs at the back, overlooked the flat above the chip shop's garden, the back bedroom window was about a foot above the ground. All external walls are about 2 feet thick traditional stone/rock and some kind of straw and mud for cement. Google Earth it, it's in Wellington Place, there are only two properties, it's easy to find. The alleyway now has a door and the chip shop on the corner is closed and its windows bricked up. To make the bathroom window that I mentioned earlier safer, I found a blacksmith who made a framework of metal bars, at the bottom was a frame so that we could put a trough in it for flowers.

The first item on the list of things to do, the day we moved in, we bought the house to include carpets. They weren't good, but at least it was something. As we entered the house we found the lounge carpet was missing. I called the estate agent, to ask where it was, we had only bare floorboards. Apparently, without asking my permission or even informing me, the police had used my house as a stakeout to watch a drug dealing house across the road. The estate agent had given them the keys to the house, I'm not sure, as I've never been told if the previous owner was aware of this either. From the way the estate agent talked I don't think they were. No one admitted it, but it could have only been the police that stole the carpet, I can't imagine for one moment that any other thief would enter the house, roll up and take away a large carpet while asking the police if they could please move off the carpet while it's being stolen. If Devon and Cornwall Police would like to deny the theft, come and see me. After some arguing, I got £150 as compensation from the estate agent, I was never told who paid it. Hardly enough to cover the cost of a new 8 x 4-metre carpet.

The next expense, but I was expecting this one, was new windows for the entire house. I knew they were quite rotten original sash windows, that the wind didn't even consider slowing down for as it whooshed through. We made the new windows special by adding leaded glass to the front of the house. The window company employed sub-contractors to fit the windows. I was supposed to pay the balance of the money to them at the end of the day when they finished. They did the most dreadful job. To fit the windows they ripped the wallpaper from around the window frames, well some they did, some they didn't. We had some windows with bare plaster around the frame, the wallpaper just ripped, not even cut, some with the wallpaper under the sealant around the windows. One window had no sealant at all, just gaps around the frame that the wind could come straight through. Not much point to double glazing if the frame isn't sealed around the edge. I refused to pay the men. They got into a right hump with me. I asked for a representative of the window company to come and look at their work. He came the next day, asking why I hadn't paid the balance as agreed. I showed him the work the sub-contractors did. He had to admit the work was quite possibly the worst he had ever seen and promised it would be made good. How they would make good the ripped wallpaper I don't know. In the end, they cut it with a knife to make a nice sharp edge instead of the ripped paper. Sealant was pumped into the finger-sized gaps around the frames that needed it. It was still a mess. As compensation, we were told the sub-contractors had been fired and would never be used again. The bathroom was very outdated, so we had a new one fitted, the company doing the fitting had problems fitting units to the walls. Three walls were actually the walls of the garden, only one wall was built of brick. Whoever built it didn't make it a cavity wall. It was literally one single line of bricks, consequently, it was very weak and one good shove it could all fall down. We didn't do anything about it, but we were aware though, not to put too much weight on it. The flat roof did leak a little, and later we would have to replace it. More on that shortly.

As I said the whole of the back of the house was underground. It seemed very damp, I guessed as it was very old there wasn't much damp course, in fact, none at all. I decided to get a company to give me a quote to do something about it. We made enquiries and got a few quotes. The company we chose seemed reasonable. Every room on the ground floor had the plaster on the wall at the back of the house removed. I had been to work and when I came home they proudly showed me their day's work. It was now all bare brick or stone. I asked why it had been necessary to hose the wall down. I was told they had not, that was how damp the wall was! We named the walls the waterfall feature. The brickwork was then, what they call, tanked. The walls were waterproofed, which consisted of painting a waterproof coat over the wall in multilayers. The brickwork remains wet but the new plaster finish would be dry. It did mean we could never drill a hole for any reason such as hanging a picture, if we did, the waterproof layer would be broken and that area would become damp. The walls were re-plastered and it all looked good. We were instructed not to paint or paper the walls for a few months to allow it to dry properly. Except, of course, this was the House of Horrors, it couldn't be that simple. A few months later, the walls began to leach out a white substance. No matter how much we cleaned it off, it kept coming back. It turns out the contractor had used sea sand in the plaster layering. It was full of salt. The salt would never stop leaching out. We could never paint the wall and there would always be a crunchy salt layer on the walls. I called the contractor, of course, they had gone bust and disappeared. Oh and because the plaster layer was now for some reason thinner, the stairs that had been attached to the wall now weren't, they were now freestanding, so as you walked up or down them, they bounced and wobbled. Good job men. In the lounge, we decided to open the closed fireplace and put in a nice gas fire that would make the room look as though we had a cosy coal fire. At the same time, I wanted to lift the floorboards and put in more electric sockets, as there was only one for the whole room. Modern times, one needs sockets for TV, video, computers, and a few spare for this and that. I lifted the floorboards in time for a contractor to come and lay the wires underneath the floor to keep it all tidy. I did the work without looking too hard underneath. I did, however, notice the house was built onto rock and, in the centre of the room, the ground literally opened into a cave that went straight down, and looking down into the hole I could see the bottom of it was water. Every time it rained, which it did that day, the hole filled up with water to a level just below the floor. We named the cave of course. In Torquay, there are very famous caves that can be visited with guided tours called Kents Cavern. We named our cave by changing one vowel in the word Kents, as our flooding cave was not particularly welcome under our lounge floor. The next day the electrician arrived to do his bit and fit the sockets around the room. He entered the room while I was in the kitchen next door. Almost immediately he came running out closing the door behind, saying he wasn't going in that room again. Why? Under the floor that I had lifted and not been too observant about it, the whole exposed area of rock was cover in 150 years of rat droppings. Some of which were still steaming. I estimated the layer of droppings was at least 6 inches deep, more in places.

Also, there were a couple of dead rats. In the rock were quite a few holes, a lot of holes, all leading under the house wall, under the alleyway in the direction of the chip shop next door. I went next door to warn the owner of the shop and to inform him that he may have a pest problem. Of course, fearing for his food retail business he denied there was ever any evidence rats came into his food shop. We called a pest control company to come to take a look. The advice was, to put poison down for the rats but they will never b completely eradicated. The only thing we could do was to put down a layer of concrete. But they will chew through the concrete and come back, so in the end, we put down a layer of broken glass first. I covered K*nts Cavern with a large thick board, laid a least three inches of broken glass over the whole area, then concreted as thick as possible to about five inches below the floorboards. The idea being, the rats will try to chew through, their guts will be shredded by the glass and they die. My good friend Susan volunteered to help. Susan was married to Marine Martin, both of whom I knew from school and were now living in Exmouth Devon about 30 miles away. Sue carried, by bucket, two tons of concrete that were dumped in the street, as there was no way the lorry could drop it directly into the room. What a tough lady, that was hard work! I fitted the new sockets myself as the electrician refused to return. The floor was re-laid. Next phase, the fireplace feature. A gas man came to look at the existing gas fire in the lounge. We were told if we ever turn it on we would probably die from the fumes. It needed replacing. The unit was standing in front of the old fireplace, which had been bricked up. We decided it would be nicer to open it up again and make a nice stone fireplace, more traditional in style. We chose a nice gas fire, that when lit looked like a real coal fire. I knocked out the bricks to the fireplace we left that whole wall as open brickwork, it was a nice look. It was ready for the fitters to come the next day to fit the new fire unit. Next morning I got up while Julie was upstairs with the kids. I went into the lounge to check all was ready for the men to arrive shortly. What I saw, Alfred Hitchcock would have been proud of. I quickly shut the door and went up to Julie. I told her not to enter the room, not to even open the door to the room to look. She thought the rats had returned already. Apparently, I didn't know this, Bluebottle flies nest, and they nest in company, 150 years' worth of Bluebottle flies had been living in the closed chimney, now I had opened it up, they had all decided to move into our lounge. Millions of them, in fact, more, that common exaggeration is an underestimate. The room was black with flies. I couldn't even see through the window, it was a moving black mass. The pest control men returned, by now they knew to help themselves to tea or coffee, they had been to our house so often. They sprayed the room, and we used buckets and shovels to clean up the dead flies.

In the kitchen, at the bottom of the wobbly stairs, was a door that led into a tiny lobby. About one square metre in size, another two doors led out. One door to the bathroom, another into the garden. Three doors in such a tiny space were awkward and like passing through an International Space Station airlock, a complicated procedure to open and close doors before one could open the next, and move on. In a tiny space, this was not good and very awkward. So, I decided to take the kitchen door out and make an arch, so the space became part of the kitchen. Now one could open the bathroom door as normal people could. I found a guy that would make an arch and plaster it up to make it nice. I would remove the door and frame and put in a lintel above where the archway would be formed to support the exterior wall above. The two feet thick wall would need at least three lintels as it was so wide, no problem, or, no problem in any other house, this was the House of Horrors. Remember I said the walls were built from rock cemented with some kind of mud and straw mix. I don't know what this type of construction is called, but it should be called crazy. If for instance, one wanted to hang a picture, a simple job in any other house. In this house, I would either hit solid rock that refused to be drilled by anything less than dynamite, or, I'd drill into the mud and straw, which would not support a sheet of toilet paper let alone a picture and frame. For this project, I needed to place the new lintels high, so that the archway could be formed below, which would be more aesthetic rather than functioning as a wall support. I removed the door frame, which turned out to be the lintel too, it held up the thick wall above, but above ground level, it was the external wall above the roof of the bathroom. Once the door frame was removed, I was expecting to find a lintel, but there was nothing to hold the wall above up, now the wooden door frame had gone. Fitted like a jigsaw puzzle, the rock that the wall was constructed of, came loose and started to fall onto me. Once one rock fell out another became loose and so on. I could only shout for help as I stood holding the 2 feet thick, 14 feet high wall up with my arms, head and shoulders to stop the whole lot from coming down. Julie came to my aid, not sure what to do, I instructed her to grab the top piece of the old, now broken, door frame and together we wedged it under the rocks to somehow hold it all up. Once I managed to get the 3 new concrete lintels into place there was a new feature to the kitchen. At night we had a nice view of the stars through the 3 feet gap between the lintels and what remained of the huge wall above. The guy that came to make the archway for me also had to first brick up the hole using the rocks that had fallen out. It all ended up well, and the new arch and 2 doors were much better than the 3 doors previously.

I noticed the roof in the bathroom was always showing signs of damp. I asked my friend Jo from school to come to stay for the weekend and help me repair the flat felt roof. He arrived Friday and together we walked around on the roof sizing up the job. We'd strip off the felt and replace it, hiring a bitumen boiler to join the layers of felt. He had done a similar DIY job for his house, so I used his expertise and knowledge. We could do the job in a weekend easily, but do you recall the name of this house? The House of Horrors, would not fail us, and there would be a surprise waiting for us of course. We stripped off the old bad felt, to leave just the wooden flat roof and joists holding it up, except, there were none. The joists, where they slotted into the back wall of the house, that was so damp before, had rotted away completely. The only thing holding up the roof was the felt we had just removed. We had been walking around on the roof that had nothing holding it up! The easy weekend job now became a complete roof rebuild. With the roof off, the one brick thick third wall (remember earlier I told you the wall had not been built as a cavity wall) became very unstable. By the end of the day, we had the old roof completely off ready to start reconstruction the next day. Overnight we had a bathroom with no roof. One could sit on the toilet and enjoy the stars, quite romantic really. Next day we started the rebuild, beginning with a long beam fixed along the top of the wobbly wall to give that some strength. We purchased all the wood and materials needed and rented a bitumen boiler. It all went quite well, the roof was made, using metal support brackets rather than just poke the joists into the recesses in the wet wall at the back, so they wouldn't rot again. Stopping for a lunch break, we forgot to turn down the boiler with the bitumen. No one noticed it start to boil, and then burst into flames. When we did discover the fire, the fire brigade had to be called to put it out. When they arrived, they made sure we had turned off the gas, and put a lid on the cauldron and stood around drinking tea, admiring our work, until the cauldron cooled enough not to reignite itself when the lid was taken off. A firefighting skill I would remember and use again soon. I discovered one of Joanne's school friend's dad, was a roofer, he volunteered to come round and inspect our work when it was finished to check we had done a good job. We passed with flying colours. Jo and his wife returned home, invigorated by the fresh, open-air showers they had taken that weekend.

I decided to fit a new kitchen. The units we had, had definitely seen better days. The project went well, apart from having huge problems hanging the wall units, as I said before it was impossible to hang anything on those walls. I think I had to fit at least 5 screw points for each cabinet, as some seemed to be screwed into the nice straw/mud. But I was becoming used to that problem now. We wanted a dishwasher. Although the kitchen room was quite big, the only place suitable was in yet another bricked up fireplace. The problem here was, not only did I have to open a fireplace, something I was very wary of now, I had to run plumbing across the room, as there was neither mains water nor drainage that side of the room. Cautiously this time, I opened up the fireplace and made sure there was a lintel to hold it all up. You can't accuse me of not learning from my mistakes. I quickly blocked off the chimney to avoid any wildlife entering that way again. The space was big enough for a dishwasher and a cupboard. The fireplace was not quite deep enough for the units, so I let them stick out a bit and put a nice shelf above to kind of hide the fact they did not fit. The plan worked quite well. I dug a channel across the concrete floor so I could fit an electricity cable, water pipes and a drain pipe to the dishwasher. That was easy, but the House of Horrors wouldn't let it be that easy. In order to send the drainpipe outside to connect to a drain, I had to drill through the 2 feet thick wall and make a 2-inch wide hole for the pipe. I swear that rock wall must be the hardest rock known to man. I had to hire a huge, what seemed to me to be like one of those giant drills you see men drilling for diamonds in mines, dropping dynamite into the hole and blowing out the mineral. I wished I had access to dynamite. The drilling machine I hired had two handles to hold while drilling. The drill bit was about 4 feet long. I sat on the kitchen floor drilling for 8 hours non-stop, to get through that wall. Occasionally the drill bit would snag on a particularly hard piece of rock and jam. The machine was so powerful, if I didn't let go quickly, it would flip me over or snap my wrists. I got through the job without breaking any bones, but I had performed a few flips that would have won me a bronze medal in gymnastics. Only a bronze medal, because the swearing that went with the flip would have lost me points.

After that, I decided the house was more or less as we wanted, by now, we quite enjoyed the bouncy stairs. So I called time on DIY. I had to redecorate every room of course, because of the mess the double glazing window fitters had left the rooms. I really needed to concentrate on the business side of things.

Having finished all that work, wouldn't it be terrible if there was a fire and we had to start all over again. My next-door neighbour, the one that didn't have any rats in his fish and chip shop, decided to help with that. One day I heard a roaring sound from the bedroom at the back of the house. I went up to see what it could be. The chip shop fryer vent exited the shop just outside our back bedroom window. It wasn't exactly quiet, but today it was like a Boeing 747 jet engine. Flames were roaring out of the vent, about 6 inches from our roof eave. The fat in the vent that had accumulated over the years was well on fire. There was a real danger it would spread into our house. I evacuated Julie and the girls. The fire brigade had been called, but they seemed to be taking their time arriving. They probably thought we had another bitumen fire or something and should be able to cope on our own having learnt how to do that. The shop owner's family were in the street, but he was nowhere to be seen. I asked where he was, his wife told me he was in the shop. I thought maybe he was overcome by the smoke and unconscious on the floor. So I dashed in. The smoke was heavy, but there was an air gap, at this point about 2 feet from the floor up to heavy thick smoke, no flames. I crawled along into the shop breathing in the air gap close to the floor, I found him stood coughing in the smoke trying to put the fryer chip oil fire out. This, in turn, had set the vent fat on fire and it was all going up in flames quite well. I told him he needed to get out before he became overwhelmed by the smoke. I have no idea what he was doing to stop the fire, he seemed to be mostly flapping around. So, having learnt previously how to extinguish oil fires in cauldrons, I made sure the gas was off, closed the fryer lids to cut off the air and dragged him out. We left the vent to burn until the firemen arrived, but turned it off so most of the air feeding the fire was cut off. I dragged him out, now having to lay flat on the floor in about 6 inches of air. Outside, the fire service was just arriving. I had only been inside for a minute at the most, my face was black, and I was blowing black snot for days after. I don't know how they put out the vent fire. But it only took a moment. They checked our roof space to make sure the fire hadn't got into our house. All was well, but it was close. I wouldn't need to start doing any DIY again, but the house never lost the smell of smoke.

After our first year in Torquay, Julie and I sat down and looked at our calendar. In the first year, we had two weekends to ourselves. We had so many visitors staying, either to help or just come and enjoy a free holiday by the sea-side. The cost of feeding our visitors was quite a strain. Don't get me wrong, we enjoyed seeing our friends, there were a few that thought they were friends, because we lived by the sea, and quite a few people were just using us. Rather than say no to people, we decided to block the spare bedrooms. So we took on students. Torquay has half a dozen language schools. In the summer the town is invaded by thousands of students from all over Europe. The schools are always appealing for homes to put them in. By doing that, when someone we could hardly remember asked if they could visit us, we could say, sorry we have no room. And the extra money was useful too.

The house always continued to present problems, no project was easy, but actually, I enjoyed it. I found the challenges and the work fun and quite therapeutic. My past was put to the back of my mind, at least for a while.

34. Business Is Good, Until...

It has been made clear to me I'm not going to be prosecuted in any way for what happened at Century House, London. MI6 cleaned it all up and made it go away. Apparently killing a spy traitor isn't frowned upon - mostly. I had saved SIS embarrassment, especially concerning the Americans, and it was all tidied up. Of course, I didn't feel good about it, but I had to move on. But I knew it would always be something SIS would use to get me to do something for them when they wanted, it would always be a dark cloud hanging over my head waiting to drop a deluge on me. A day would soon come when I thought the deluge had arrived.

During the time I am occupied with the house, I'm also working at the factory. The deal with the previous owner signed sealed and delivered. It was going ok, a few problems here and there and I think I did a fair job at bringing the business into the 20th century, slowly turnover began to rise.

For recreation, of course, living by the sea there had to be sailing. I went to Torquay Harbour where there were a few shops to asked around. I was in a chandler shop, asking if they knew anyone that needed crew. Luck had it, at that moment Ted was in the shop and he overheard me asking. Ted had a half share in a yacht with Mike his friend (and soon to become my new best friend) and was looking for crew. I was invited to join them on the Wednesday evening club yacht race in Torbay with the Royal Torbay Yacht Club (RTYC). I must have shown myself to be worthy as I was invited back the following week to crew for them again. More on this later.

Back at work, things were going fine. I resolved the 'invoice once a year' problem by sending out invoices monthly and offering a discount to any company that wanted to pay within thirty days. Most took advantage of the offer, some didn't. Those that didn't the following year had their bill loaded, the price list for them was higher. In my mind, a customer that doesn't want to pay isn't a customer. I had a big range of customers, spread about 50% retail outlets, and 50% boat hire companies, of those, most of them were on the Norfolk Broads. Retail businesses would order between 10 and 20 buoyancy aids, and the hire companies would order between 10 and 50, generally. When I first took over the business, the staff were all on piecework, meaning they were given a pile of work, let's say 50 jackets to sow in a day, and they were paid an amount per jacket. What tended to happen was once their pile was finished they would pack up and go home. I wanted to change this to get a full day's work from them. With their agreement, I paid them an hourly wage, slightly higher than the piecework rate. That way, I could ask them to sow, then maybe do a bit of packing, or anything else. I think they enjoyed the variety too. We became more of a family and they always helped out if I needed it. I did all the office work myself, and every day did work in the workshop. I'm a strong believer in the "never ask someone to do something I'm not prepared to do myself" philosophy (well, there is one exception, sorry ladies). It also meant they could look after themselves if I needed to go out for a few days to attend a trade show (something the previous owner never did) or meetings. It was all going well, and I think the staff appreciated that I would muck in too.

One day, to my huge surprise, and horror, I had a visitor to the factory. John, my mentor walked in. Good to see him again, but not. Amazingly, John had a business in Torquay too. Of all the places we could be! John had a small camera shop and photo developing company in the main shopping street in town. In those days, before digital, you had to take a roll of film to be developed and printed - children. Anyhow, John had heard I made things for boats, he wanted a cover for his surfboard. We made one for him. Slightly wary there could be something more to this coincidence I started visiting John in his shop, we'd be in the back of his shop with a cup of tea, nattering while he and his staff did the film processing. Quite a useful job, you get the chance to see everyone's photos. It's amazing how many people weren't shy about sending in their "bedroom" pictures for development, we had quite a few childish giggles. John and I became better friends and once a month we took it in turns to host a dinner party, Julie and I and John his partner Janet. Janet was a rep for a soft toy company. Janet and John lived in the centre of Totnes. Totnes if you don't know it is the country's centre for the hippy community. All things weird go on there. Last time I looked there were approximately 170 alternative medicine centres in the town. Most quite cranky, such as dancing in a circle naked while banging a tambourine. I hope I'm not one to criticise, if that makes you feel better, then it's good, isn't it? Anyway, John was taking the hippy atmosphere too much to heart, I think the tobacco in his roll-ups had a very strange smell to them. But, he also sailed on a yacht at RTYC, so we had at least something in common. At least now we started to have a circle of friends in Devon, life was mostly good, but, then I started to get wind of good, yet bad news.

Downsouth (Torquay) Ltd was a member of the British Marine Industries Federation (BMIF). This was a source of information and all things in the marine industry. One such thing was, each year the jackets I, and all UK companies that manufactured buoyancy aids and life jackets, submitted our products for testing in BMIF laboratories. This meant each of our jackets were tested and proven to work as they should, i.e. the person should float face up. I had to send one jacket for each of the six sizes every year to be tested. I never had a fail. It was proposed, that a new test, for a European Standard, be set up. This was good because it unified all of Europe's, buoyancy aids and life jackets. This would mean our market would be opened up to sell in Europe and not just Britain. Until now, if I wanted to sell in any other country, I would have to get my jackets tested to each individual country's standards. It sounded good, the trouble is, whenever our government, and even more so, Europe, is involved, things do not and never can be smooth working (Brexit is a fine example). The proposal to unify, was good, but by the end, I realised in fact, it must have been more about destroying any industry. No one could decide what those new regulations would be. It dragged on, and on, and on. Every country had its own idea. A date was set when the new regulations would come into force, from memory it was July 1994, but my memory isn't the best, I'm probably wrong on that. But let's say for now it was that date. In my business I planned a year in advance what I was going to do the following year, trying to predict sales and ordering materials accordingly. In late 1993 nothing was yet decided regarding the EU regulations for the marine industry. I didn't know how to plan. I saw a draft copy of the regulations, which gave me some clues and it was going to be a disaster. For instance. For my jackets to be tested each year, now they would have to be tested by someone else, a new laboratory for the whole of Europe, no one knew who yet. And as a for instance, the plan was, in the draft proposal, for each Jacket type, I had one type, each size, I had six sizes, had to be water tested. They always were. But now each size, let's say the size for a 12 stone person, had to be tested by six different shape people, a tall thin man, a short fat man, and so on. So for my six sizes, I would need to find 36 different shaped people willing to put on my jacket and jump in a pool to see if they floated. There were nine other businesses in the UK manufacturing life jackets of some kind. Each of them would need to do the same. Another example of the future of testing would be that the material used had to be of a certain quality, and numbers were in the draft saying what that quality was. I phoned my material suppliers, none of them knew or had heard what the material was, I could not buy anything for the new regulations because no one had heard of the type of material needed. Until 1993 the cost of testing was, for my company in round numbers, £1000. Using the draft regulations the manufacturing companies in the UK estimated the cost for me would become £32,000. I couldn't afford that, neither could any other company in the UK. I had buyers calling me wanting to place orders to the new standards, I had to tell them we didn't know what they were yet, sales dropped. The same was happening to all the other manufacturers in the UK, probably Europe. It was a total mess. In the end, I decided we could not continue to operate under such conditions. That year every manufacturing company in the UK, most of them bigger than my little business, closed down and ceased trading. Europe had killed the industry, well-done people.

It wasn't all bad news, one wise Norfolk Broad Boat Hire owner saw the industry was having problems and placed the biggest order ever, 650 jackets. We completed the order before I announced to the staff we could not continue in business with the regulations in chaos.

After working at my own business for almost five years, I had to announce to my good, loyal staff, to pack up their things and go home. They had all worked hard with me and it was a day I won't forget, ever. As for me, working hard had helped me put my past to the back of my mind. Outside of work the DIY, my children, fantastic wife and sailing had meant all in all I had a great life, and now, it was all shattered again.

What was to happen soon changed my life, my way of thinking, my depression. Three separate events, years apart none the less, finally ended all the secrets and lies. But before I tell you about those two important events, I will tell you about another business that happened quite by accident.

35. Another Business

I had always wanted to have a house in Spain. So Julie and I decided to make it come true Julie stayed at home with the children, while I went with a friend to house hunt. I had details on several farms around the town of Gandesa, Catalan Spain. About an hour's drive south from Barcelona to Tarragona, then turn right and head inland for an hour to the lovely wine region. It was quite remote and quiet, so property prices were very cheap. Once we had looked at a few it became apparent a farm was not going to be suitable. What was described as a house on a packet of land, would turn out to be nothing more than a shed. With no electricity or water, but some had an underground cisterna. Apparently, some farmers have a house in town and go into the countryside to their farm and sleep on a cot returning home at the weekend. It was not suitable at all for a home. There was no chance of any planning permission to build a house. So I asked the estate agent to come up with some townhouses instead. We looked at a few, some nice and ready to move into, some complete wrecks needing restoration. I quite liked a house in a small village called La Pobla de Massaluca in the middle of nowhere. It had a population of about 250 people and I would be the first foreigner to buy a house there. It needed a bit of work but it was liveable, had electricity, water and gas from a cylinder, like most houses in Spain. It was in a perfect location just off a small square in the centre of the village, with a couple of shops and a bar just across the road. It had been up for sale for four years after the elderly lady that lived there died. I put in an offer and it was accepted. I hoped it wasn't going to be another money pit. In the end, it proved to be the opposite. In all, including taxes, rates, electricity, water and gas it cost me £250 per year to keep it going. Anytime we had a few spare days we would go there, flying from England to either Barcelona or Reus airport, renting a car and driving the 2 hours to our house. The kids hated it. It was too quiet and far from the nearest beach. Often I'd go by myself to do some work on the house or with Mike for boy's time out. We had so much fun and the locals were fantastic lovely people.

On the trip to house hunt, my daughters had asked me to bring home a present for them. I found some gorgeous porcelain dolls for them. A few months down the line one of the dolls was accidentally broken, and I promised to find another for them. I looked everywhere for one, I could not find anyone that sold them in England, so I called the company that made them in Spain. A company called Bubinots. I asked them if anyone sold them in England, I was told no, only in Spain. On the spur of the moment, I asked if they would like someone to sell them for them in England. They said, yes, they'd love that, so, I jumped on a plane and drove to Cerdanyola just north of Barcelona and met the owners at the pottery. I was shown around the factory and met the nice lady that designed the models. There were about 250 different models in the range. I came home with an agreement that I would have sole rights to sell Bubinots for the whole of the UK, as well as a replacement figure for the girls. I had done no due diligence, business plan or anything. Bubinots UK was born. I started selling at several gift trade shows. I designed and made a trade stand, brochures and price lists and just got on with selling them. It took a couple of years to get established and I was just getting to the stage where a couple of big mail order catalogue companies were becoming interested in contracts. I loved it, I loved going to the trade shows, it was like a moving community of people, we'd meet the same people at every show and got to know a few, so we were never alone in the evenings.

After a couple of years, just before a trade show in the Riviera Centre in Torquay, I made a call to Spain. I liked to warn them I was doing a show to prepare them for orders. The thing the British like is fast prompt delivery, the thing the Spanish like is the opposite. I called to tell them to prepare for an order after the show that needed to be delivered very quickly. The pottery was quite reasonable and was always helpful. On this occasion it was different. "We have a problem Andy" I was told, "the pottery has closed, we have gone bust". I couldn't believe it, yet again a business that I have worked hard to become successful and profitable will have to close through no real fault of mine. I spoke to the designer of the models, she promised to fulfil the orders that I will get at the trade show. She also promised that she wanted Bubinots to continue and would find a new pottery manufacturer.

After the show, I had quite a few orders, and as promised the orders were sent to me. They actually cut the chains on the doors of the factory and stole all the figures I needed from the official receiver.

As promised the designer found a new pottery manufacturer. The pottery parts were made in Portugal now, then sent back to Spain to be painted by hand and assembled. The problem was this made them too expensive to sell. I told them so. They asked me to give them a price that I thought I could sell them for. I produced a price list for every single one of the 250 models. I was told they could not even make them for the prices I set, let alone wholesale them. So once again my little business folded. I sold my stock of Bubinots, and, the only business I've had since I left SIS that I enjoyed, closed.

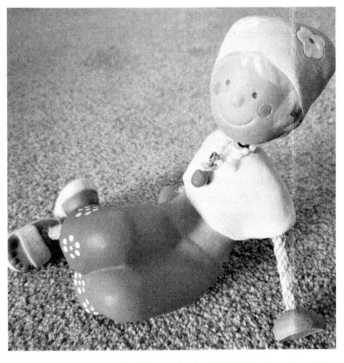

Figure 6. One of the original Bubinots bought while house hunting in Spain

36. Event 1. Deep Depression

The next few months were pure hell. I had to deal with the closure of my Downsouth buoyancy aid factory, without any advice or help from anyone. Not only was the physical aspects of shutting down, and disposal of the assets, but the mental strain upon me huge. I had a young family to feed, a home to keep for them, plus the financial pressures that placed on me I could feel was moving me back into depression. Not all the decisions I made were good. I also had to figure out what to do for work. I didn't want to work for anyone and join the morning trudge into a job where I'm expected to give my life to enhance some faceless fat cat's share dividend.

I found a company that made portable ball pools, so I purchased one, to rent it out for children's parties. I went, reluctantly, to a local printer and offered my services to work at home doing any typesetting they could not cope with, by computer. I seemed to be one of the first in Devon to find the software needed to do that, Devon always being about ten years behind the rest of the world. Surprisingly, I became quite busy with both little businesses, but I enjoyed neither. I just didn't know what to do. I made enquiries through John about returning to SIS. I'd been out of the loop for years, but with the contacts I knew I could restore, I thought I might be able to be useful for something. I tried to prove my point by passing information on a few local drug smugglers which I believed would give me some credit back at London. All that happened was, and actually would be quite normal usually, after a couple of our country's biggest drug seizures in Torbay, the local police alongside MI5 took all the credit, the information that I supplied to them to enabled them to find the hauls of contraband was used, but I was overlooked. I wouldn't mind being overlooked as a spy, it was quite usual to remain incognito, but I seemed to be overlooked in order to win favour back into SIS. I did manage to get an interview in London. Faces had changed, I had changed. I had picked up the Devon way of life without realising it. I was too laid back, I didn't let life rush me. I failed the interview dismally. In particular the psychological tests, again. The Head of MI6 was now Sir Colin McColl, who, I didn't know at all. That was about to change and John Scarlett was about to become Head, I just didn't know anyone or the new technology now being used. MI6 had even moved out of Century House, into the now very famous and very visible property at Vauxhall Cross, the building seems to have acquired several nicknames as well as appearing in films and TV. Life in the spy business had changed so much in the five years I had been out of it. Spying mostly seemed to be on screen, there were rows of computer monitors and the business was conducted by computer from secretly installed cameras everywhere. I had little to nothing to win me back into the club known as MI6, and, probably if I had, I could not have done much or would have been very bored in this new modern computer led world. MI6 had become very public and visible, a move probably very necessary in order, by public demand, to continue to receive proper funding in a sad new world of budget cuts.

My resignation had never been formally accepted, yet, I wasn't in receipt of any payments or salary from SIS, I realised I was in this lost middle world. Still subject to the

Official Secrets Act, still subject to bank account checks and my movements being watched, but kept out of the main game. I assumed if ever cannon fodder was needed, that would be the time they'd come get me to help, they knew where I lived.

In the end and with kind permission from my ever tolerant wife Julie, I decided to do nothing much with my life for a year. To just relax, try to get my head together and figure out what to do for work eventually. I did nothing very successfully, the ball pool rental business was ticking over without little effort from me. I did typesetting when I was asked by the printing business over the road from our house. In the end, the year turned into two.

We had given up on the money pit house in Ellacombe. We could not afford to keep pumping money into it to keep it standing. We let it go, and for now, we rented a big house in Newton Abbot. John's ex-wife's sister's third cousin, or something like that, had a house rental business and found us a real bargain of a house to rent. I spent far too much time sailing. Ted and Mike invited me to join them, with the rest of their crew, to enter as many yacht races as we could. There was race night on Wednesdays and Sunday mornings at RTYC in Torbay. Coastal races with the club too. Thursday evening was race night at Brixham Yacht Club, we'd sail over the bay to Brixham and join the races there too. After a race, we'd go ashore and enjoy the fantastic views across the bay from the Yacht Club bar, enjoying superb food and good beer, sailing home late in the evening, slightly merry and probably in an unsafe condition for the trip back to Torquay by boat. Ted and Mike changed yachts from the one-design racer they shared to a beautiful Sigma 33. This meant we could now sail further and cross the English Channel, sleeping on board. We entered numerous races around the area, a fantastic experience and, at very little cost to me. One such race was the Sigma Europeans in Guernsey, joining yachts from all over Europe in a large fleet. In our first race I earned, after a mistake rigging the spinnaker sail, the nickname Andy Sideways. Somehow I connected the halyard and sheets onto the wrong points of the sail and it went up in all its colour, sideways.

The fun we had and the experience I gained was fantastic. I earned Ted and Mike's trust, and on occasions when they could not make race nights for whatever reason, they would ask me to take the boat out for them, in order to maintain our race series score. One year, in a possible thirteen race cups, we won eleven.

Eventually, though it had to end. Ted and Mike were constantly arguing about costs. Yachts aren't cheap, and their partnership in the yacht was dissolved. Ted was becoming more unfit. As an ex-second world war bomber pilot, he had many tales to tell of his life in the RAF, yet always modest, I had to wring the stories out of him. His bravery in the war was an inspiration, it was sad to see him get too old to sail, which was all he lived for. He died a few years ago and I miss his knowledge and slightly cookie advice.

Mike, however, was ex-Navy. A few years older than me, we got on very well and continued our friendship. We would go out with our wives every week for a meal somewhere, visiting the many restaurants in and around Torbay. Fed up of not having anything to sail, Mike asked me if I would like to join him in a partnership in a boat. I declined because one, I could not ensure my finances would be predictable and two, I saw how boat partnerships result in arguments, always, about money. He noticed a poor old boat in Torquay Marina up for sail. It had been neglected for years, and, with the mooring fees unpaid, was taken into possession by the Marina Company and put up for auction. He won it, with his bid at £750, he was now the proud owner of a 23 foot Irish built one-design yacht, attached to the bottom of the sea by seaweed growing from under the boat. He asked me to help him restore the boat. I agreed to help but I wanted no part in the ownership or cost. He agreed, which was great. We worked together for two years restoring the boat almost full time. Mike was a taxi driver in Torquay. After two years of not doing much in the way of work, he also asked me if I would like to rent a car from him. Which I did. Together we would play at boat restorers during the day, and work at night. In a week I would sleep probably three nights. It was fun and I acquired a lot of new skills, with Mike supplying the ideas and money, me doing the work, while he made the tea or coffee.

This should have been the perfect life, but for me, it wasn't. My memories and guilt were forever playing games in my head. Despite the fun and great way of life we had, I was becoming more and more depressed. Julie wanted to buy another house, but we could not get a mortgage, I hadn't been working in the taxi business long enough to have good account records. I became deeply depressed that I could not provide a nice home for my family and relative security for them. We tried very hard, and it prayed on me. I tried to cover it all up by playing boats. Julie seemed to be completely unaware of my feelings, I was at fault for not telling her, even hinting at the real reason. I was just scared to tell my wife that I was a man that she knew nothing about, beyond that which she saw and I permitted her to see each day. My guilt and inability to think about what I should be doing with my life prayed heavily on me, in the end, I cracked again.

I took one ibuprofen and one paracetamol, a combination that always helps me to sleep easily. On my driveway, I sat in my car with a hosepipe from the exhaust fed inside the car, and I sat in peace waiting for it all to end. I was finally peaceful and calm, I knew now the images and guilt I always had in my head every minute of the day would be gone. I would join Filipe and his wife, even though I knew them for such a short moment in time I owed them an apology. My eyes closed my thoughts drifted into a happy place. So peaceful at last.

I woke up in a bright place, out of focus people were fussing around me sticking needles into me, I heard someone say "Petrol fumes are ok, it's diesel that is carcinogenic".

Really! I was in Torbay Hospital with a multitude of tubes and wires stuck into me, so many I could not move. Apparently, Julie came home early from work, found me in the car and 'saved' me. This wasn't the plan. My brain came back into focus. Damn it! I'm still alive. Is there ever going to be an end to my turmoil? I hadn't given this part any thought, I have no plans for my future. How could I face Julie, I'd hurt her yet again, she didn't deserve me. I spent a couple of days in the hospital, 'getting better' before I was moved by ambulance, accompanied by some kind of heavy bodyguard, to Newton Abbot Hospital, literally 400 yards from my house in East Street. The hospital has since been knocked down and replaced by a modern new one. The original one where I was taken to was an old Victorian building. There was a ward for people like me. I have no idea what the ward was called, but it was secure, the people inside could not get out, nor could anyone get in without passing through some kind of security system. Here, I was told that the government doesn't like people trying to end their life, and therefore takes over the responsibility to help restore sanity. I saw the great irony in that statement, my government had asked me many times to risk my life for them and the people of my country, now I'm being told they care!

The ward, if I can call it that, was actually very nice. Clean, fresh, bright and airy with a nice garden to sit in. It was more like a hotel, with nice food and a kitchen where one could make a tea or coffee. I had a room to myself, all the patients did, just like a hotel room. I was put on suicide watch, which basically meant someone followed and watched me every moment of the day and sat outside my room at night occasionally peeping through the window in the door to check on me. There were male and female bedroom wards because our government doesn't like men and women sleeping in rooms next to each other either. The staff were kind, probably most of them lived in Totnes hippy town, but they were absolutely useless, I would describe them as a teapot with no spout, unfit for purpose. Compared to the private doctors I saw in SIS and those at RAF Halton Hospital, these NHS people had absolutely zero clue how to help their patients. Yes, they could happily follow me around all day, but that was it, they didn't seem to know how to talk. None of them spoke to me, I don't know why. I was given a welcome to Newton Abbot Hospital speech, explaining the rules of the house, which, basically told me not to go into the women's sleeping quarters. Apart from that, I was free to wander into the common room or do some art in the art room with no paint or paper. There was a television and a tiny room with an ancient computer that had almost no useful programs.

Each day I had to go for a 'chat' with a psychologist but his title should have been psychopath, he did not seem to understand how to deal with someone like me at all, and, for sure he underestimated my intelligence. We sat in a room alone on beanbags, all very Totnesy, I wondered if we should get naked and bang tambourines, it may have worked better than his line of chat. He would ask me interesting questions, such as:

"How are you feeling today Andy?"

"I'm fine thank you, lovely hotel you have here"

"Are you feeling better today?"

"Better than what?"

"Well, do you think your life is better today?"

"How can it be better I'm stuck in here, I need to go home to make things better with my wife"

"How would you make it better?"

"I have no idea, if I knew the answer to that, I probably would not be here"

Apparently, that was the wrong answer, by not having a plan to make things better, meant I had to remain in this secure unit for longer, it took me a while to realise that, but I did not understand the logic of the questions. I did not have any clue how to make my life better, to get the negative thoughts out of my head, I hadn't planned to be around to necessitate devising a plan.

Another day another interesting chat with the clueless idiot.

"How are you feeling today Andy?"

"I'm fine thank you, lovely hotel you have here"

"Are you feeling better today?"

"Better than what?"

"Well, do you think your life is better today?"

"How can it be better I'm stuck in here, I need to go home to make things better with my wife"

"How would you make it better?"

"Bang some tambourines and dance naked"

I still hadn't found the right answer, so every day I would just tell everyone that I just wanted to go home. I have no idea what this was doing to Julie, it must have been so awful for her, how could I do this to her. I needed a plan. The plan came to me after I had been playing on the computer in the little room one day. The only game on the ancient thing was minesweeper, I played it for hours as there was little else to do, other than making tea or coffee. It was nice to sit in the garden, especially as it was good sunny weather, the fresh air and the freedom this gave me was comforting. One day as I left the computer room, my suicide watcher was outside in the corridor, as I passed her, I commented that the game was difficult to win, just for something to say to my otherwise silent follower. She must have taken my comment as something negative and upsetting to me, because the next time I went to play, I found the computer room was locked and they would not let me in to play again. That was it for me, boredom if nothing else would make me go crazy, in this house for crazy people. It was time to get myself out.

I went to my room to think, I lay on my bed and made a plan, a plan that would show these fuck wits who I was, what I was capable of, that I could outwit them easily and, I would use all the skills taught to me at Spy School.

While I was laying on my bed alone in my room thinking, I also timed how often the face would appear at my door window to check I was not harming myself. I got it, and my plan was complete. It took me two days to get everything into place, I was ready to show these idiots who they were dealing with. Julie came to visit, we sat in my room, I couldn't say sorry enough to her. I also asked her for a couple of pounds as I wanted to buy something and I needed her to bring some things for my plan, but I didn't tell her what I was preparing. She didn't question how I was going to buy something as there was no shop in the hospital, well, there may have been somewhere, but I had no access to it in this ward.

Keep in mind, all the time I am putting my plan into place to get out, I am being followed and watched. My day started as normal, I got out of bed, washed and dressed and went for breakfast as I had every day. After which, I had a few minor pieces to my plan to complete at the last minute. I was ready to show them all. About 11 am, coffee time, I made myself a coffee in the kitchen and went back to my room to drink alone, I sat on my bed, occupied myself doing puzzles in a puzzle book Julie had bought me, I had the money she bought in my pocket ready. I waited until I saw the face appear at the door window, as soon as it disappeared I sprang into action, two days of secret planning was about to come to fruition.

Ten minutes later, the face appeared at the window, I was gone. I can only guess at the panic that must have ensued by my disappearance.

Thirty minutes later, I reappeared, I was standing quite calmly, at their office door in the ward, watching all the staff panicking, they were trying to figure out where I had gone. I was wet with sweat from the physical exertion I had just put myself through, but they didn't notice. They were so intent on flapping their arms or whatever, they didn't even see me standing there, so I spoke.

"Would anyone like a sweet?" I asked them. I held out a packet of sweets, offering them one of the sweets I'd just bought.

"Where have you been? We were just about to call the police to search for you" the head idiot answered.

"I went into town, I fancied some sweets, and I'm back now. Did you read the note I left on my bed?"

"Yes, it said you have left a message on the computer and you will be back shortly"

"Yes, so what's the problem? I'm back"

The head idiot led me away fuming, and I mean fuming, there was real smoke coming out his ears. He led me into the chat room with beanbags almost screaming.

"Calm down, mate," I said to him, giggling to myself inside. "You read my note and it said I had left a message on the computer, did you read the message?"

"No, they can't figure out how to turn on the computer". Fuck it, there is no end to their stupidity.

"Well, the message says, I have just popped into town to get some sweets and I will be back shortly, what's the problem?"

"You cannot leave without our permission, we have to monitor you"

I went on to explain the whole thing to the idiot.

"So, let me tell you what's just happened. Under your monitoring and supervision, I have entered a locked room and left a message on the computer you no longer allow me to use. I have exited the building without you or security seeing me go. I have re-entered the building after buying this packet of sweets from a shop in town without you seeing me come back into the building. Not only that, but I have also stolen every knife from the kitchen if you go look. I have hidden those knives all over the ward, they are in plant pots, under people's beds, down the side of chairs, they are everywhere. Now, you see, now you know what I can do, while under your watchful eyes, I am capable of more, much more. If you think this was trouble, just wait and see what else I am capable of. I strongly suggest you let me go home now, or you will have problems like you never imagined."

The packet of sweets was purely to prove I had been into town. The poor guy would have been speechless if he had any sense, but he wanted to shout at me, so I let him, but I was not fazed by his rant at all. I can't recall what he was shouting about, I was not listening. I was adamant I was going to go home. I made it quite clear to him, I could make trouble for him and the best thing he could do for me was to let me go home.

Two hours later Julie arrived to take me home.

We arrived home and I was happy to be there. She sat me down and made me promise never to do anything like that ever again, never to try to take my life again. She couldn't figure out how I had convinced them to let me come home either. I promised and I meant it.

The most important thing to me was, my inner confidence had grown, I had won the war against those so-called experts, and I knew I could still do it when necessary and that was stage one of my recovery.

Life after that took a turn for the better, and worse. The fun I had outwitting the so-called, experts in the hospital just filled me with confidence and deep inside a pride, that I still had it, I don't know what I had, but from that moment I knew, I was smarter and cleverer than people that call themselves experts. But, I was very unhappy that I had treated Julie so badly. In my mind, it was all about me, my problems, my thoughts and my memories that haunted me every day. Those events and another that was about to happen would change my entire life. I had promised Julie I would not try anything stupid such as cowardly suicide ever again. I intended to keep that promise with all my heart. I had hurt her enough, but for me to stop hurting her, I had to break from her. It seemed like more cruelty and more hurt, but it was the only way. I decided she would be better off without me. After all, if I had been successful in killing myself she would be without me, and that was the only way, in the long run, to make her happy. She could never be happy living with me. Maybe it was very wrong of me to decide such a huge issue alone, but I knew she would never want me to leave her. That is not vanity talking, it was the truth. I was always going to be off sailing or being depressed, and I could never bring myself to tell her that the real reason was that she slept next to a killer. That my entire life was secret from her and she didn't deserve that, she was the most perfect wife and she didn't deserve me and my problems.

Quite possibly the most selfish person I could be, I decided I could not stay and give her the problems I knew I caused. I'd find somewhere else to go and she would, in time, make a new life and she would be successful and happier, it was obvious. Sometimes you have to be cruel to be kind. I knew she would be hurt again, but in the long run, in my opinion, it was best for her.

It took me a couple of years to plan another life. I didn't tell anyone what I was up to. I planned to leave and go far far away and hide like a coward so that I did not have to watch her suffer, which she probably did, a lot. I saw her cry like I never saw anyone cry, proper, deep inside and out crying. She told me she didn't want me to go, but I had to, it was the only way. I left hurting that I had to do it to her, but I could see no other way forward for her. She had done nothing wrong, ever.

37. Event 2 and 3. Goodbye John And Dad

Julie and I had separated and our divorce was in progress. I went to live temporarily in a share house. There were four people living in the house in Torquay, I hated every moment of it. I had planned to move far away from, I would say everything and everyone, but in reality, I was running from myself. I only had myself to blame for what happened, in every aspect of my life. I had planned to go live in the Philippines. I would go once my divorce was settled. I now felt more confident in myself after the hospital escape. The only way forward, as I saw it, was to move far away and hide, mostly from my guilt.

In the room next to mine in the share house was a lovely lady, 5'3" blond, great figure, whenever I saw her she was always smiling, she never seemed to be unhappy. She was Lithuanian born, Jurate. From day one living in the house, clearly, I must have looked dreadful, I don't know if it was pity or what, but Jurate for some reason always made sure I had some food, she made amazing dinners, always too much for herself, and so, gave me a share. We spent some time together and I learnt her story, she could write a book about her life, maybe she will one day. We spent more and more time together.

It wasn't part of my plan to be with someone in England, I had plans in place in Mindanao Island, Philippines, where a house and small shop was waiting for me. There was also a lovely lady Malou and family waiting for me to become part of their life. I also planned to do a short course in Bayugan, Mindanao to learn how to keep pigs. The garden of the house was big enough for eight pigs. That and the shop would keep me busy and with some income to live in reasonable poverty until I could take my pension.

Jurate and I became closer and spent more and more time together. It was obvious we were becoming an 'item'. There would be a danger, if I wasn't careful, that she would scupper my plans to live in Bayugan, I wasn't careful. I did some tentative checks on her as being Lithuanian meant she had a Russian upbringing. I found out there was a possibility that at least one member of her family in Lithuania was KGB. This was nothing unusual, almost everyone in Russian countries had to report on neighbours or even family if that person was not towing the Communist line. Jurate herself was a signed-up member of the Communist party. But the way it works there is, you sign up, you get a better job and a better living. I was assured she was simply making her life easier for herself. In fact, this seemed to be true, as she had a job as manager of a brewery in Kaunas before she had to leave. She also had a bar somewhere in the woods outside Kaunas, by the river Nemunas. She stole beer from the brewery to stock her bar. I was worried she could be some kind of honey trap, but in the end, everything she told me about herself seemed to pan out. Her story is more amazing than mine, why she had to leave her home, got barred from America, and came to live in England, she even had her car blown up by the mafia before she left.

One day she went off to work, my room next to hers was small, single bed size. She had said many times her dream was to live in a house with a walk-in wardrobe. I decided to make her dream come true. The moment she left for work, I emptied my bedroom of all the furniture, putting it all in the garage. I had some stand-alone shelving from the Bubinots trade show stand. I erected the shelving around the perimeter of my room, got into her room, emptied all her wardrobe and clothes drawers and made my room into her walk-in-wardrobe dream. Jurate had so many clothes it took me all day to fold and place them onto the shelves, all sorted into shirts, tops, dresses, jumpers, etc., etc. Eight hours I spent folding everything using a ruler to get them all uniform in size. The end result looked like some kind of posh shop. I finished about thirty minutes before she returned from work. I met her at the door as she came in, and told her I had a surprise for her. I took her to our rooms and opened the door to what was my old room and now a walk-in wardrobe. She was impressed I think. The downside, I told her was that I now had nowhere to sleep. We have been together ever since. We married 4th November 2011.

This did, unfortunately, mean I now had to drop my plans to go live in the Philippines. I had to, yet again, hurt someone very kind, intelligent and beautiful and had done nothing wrong, in fact, had done everything right. I let down Malou and her family, they had done so much to prepare the way for me to live with them. What followed was the event that made me tell everything to Jurate. With predictable results.

In 2011 we went to Spain for a holiday. I was in a happy place. Sitting in the garden of the villa in the gorgeous sun, by the pool, sipping a cold beer, there was an unexpected buzz on my phone. A message arrived, it was John, my ex-mentor, and friend. I had not been in touch with anyone or anything SIS for a long time. So this was a shock. I immediately thought this was the call, they needed some cannon fodder somewhere and it was time to call Andy. I was wrong. It was bad news. Karen had died. She passed away from cancer. I hadn't seen her for so many years, I had no idea. We had drifted apart, had never said goodbye, or even 'see you later'. The most beautiful, smart, funny lady I have ever known has gone. All the memories that I had locked away somewhere in the vaults of my brain flooded out, the visions of her beauty, Filipe lying dead, the lies to Julie and everyone in my life, the shooting of Jean, the pictures in my brain suddenly came back into the front of my head. Pictures of pieces of Jean's brain splattering on the wall behind her. Everything bad all at once. I burst into tears, crying like a baby, I couldn't help it. I thought I had all this locked away, and now it came back in a rush. Why didn't anyone think to tell me Karen was ill? Jurate came out into the garden from the villa and saw me. "What's wrong with you, what's happened, we are in the most beautiful place and you are crying?" she asked.

"Give me a minute" I left the garden and sat in the bedroom for a moment to compose myself. I returned a message to John. He didn't give me any information, he just didn't realise Karen and I were so close I suppose. I asked if it was ok to tell Jurate the real reason I was upset. I had decided enough was enough and from now on I wanted to be honest to Jurate, and, everyone. Somehow I knew by telling her the truth it would help me. Maybe then I could share some of my burdens and it would help, I just knew I had to tell, I didn't want to lie to anyone any more. John asked me to wait a moment while he checked with a higher authority about my request. It didn't take too long for the reply. It was fine to tell anyone I wanted, so long as I never pass on any of the secret stuff. I should have guessed they knew how this would go down with friends and family, I should have guessed too.

I returned to the garden, sat in the sun by the pool and told Jurate everything. When I was finished, she simply said "I don't believe you" and walked away.

Those four words have been true for almost everyone I have told. Too many lies and secrets and the mere fact that I got away with the lies for so long making my story 'unbelievable'.

I've told my best friends and some colleagues. After telling a few people and got very mixed and odd reactions from them, I slowed down the rate of my honesty. I was happy I finally got it all out into the open, it helps me tremendously with my own personal mental health.

John was always a bit of a problem for me. As a mentor, he was bloody useless. When I first started work at MI6 his mentoring technique was that I should learn by mistakes. In my mind, the world of espionage and spying is too dangerous to make mistakes, so I made sure I didn't make any. Maybe that was his reasoning, I felt it was in order for me to fail. When he first appeared in Torquay at my factory to ask for a cover for his surfboard to be made to measure, that was never a coincidence, and then to join the yacht club, that was obvious he was keeping me under observation, even more, he was hounding me deliberately so that I knew, always, I was being watched closely. The secret world I had lived and worked in doesn't like members of its family going their own way. Richard Tomlinson was the most public example of that. He did give away some secrets in his memoirs, and he went to prison for it. On his release, he was hounded wherever he went. Whatever country he tried to make a new life in he was forced to move on, in the hope one day he will decide it's easier to end his life, and that would be a great example to others not to do the same thing. The resources and effort put into that kind of hounding, in my opinion, is disproportionate. I left the business under totally different conditions, I didn't leave to make some political point. In 2018 it was thirty years since I had to quit the service. The cost of keeping an eye on me to the taxpayer was ridiculous in my opinion. I am not a traitor, or another Peter Wright or Richard Tomlinson, my memoirs do not give away any secrets, ok maybe letting the world know MI6 has spies inside the UN is close to that, but it must be obvious to anyone that they probably have spies inside all big organisations, and so does every other country. But thirty years of having strange clicks on my phone, mail obviously opened and resealed, my home entered and searched when I'm away. Yes, I know they do that and I feel violated. 2018 was the year to put an end to that.

Jurate and I were at a car boot one Sunday, its Jurate's favourite pastime, she calls it her church as it's every Sunday in the summer, she tells her manager at work she needs to have Sundays off to go to church, she is a chef at a popular restaurant open 7 days a week. We were walking around the car boot, on a Sunday morning it's a huge one on the ring road at Paignton, our next-door neighbour passed us, stopped us and asked "Did you see anything strange last night"

"No, Such as what" I replied, he looked perturbed,

"We saw a man dressed in black pass through our garden through the gate into your garden. I raced out after him, but, by the time I got outside he was gone".

Our garden is the middle of a row of three. His garden was at the end where the road passes by the side. There is a gate from his into ours because before we moved in the previous occupier was in the Navy, away for months at a time, so, Alan our neighbour would come through the gate to cut his grass for him while he was away. The gate had been put in for that purpose.

"No, we were watching TV, we didn't see a thing, how strange". Yes, it was strange and I took a good guess why. We never close our lounge curtains of the window that looks out into our garden. It's part of my PTSD, I need to be able to see outside, even when it's dark. I don't sleep with my bedroom door closed either, and can only sleep facing the door, I get very edgy if I have my back to the door, it's something I have to live with. If anyone is in our garden they can see us clearly in our home. There is no purpose to this other than scare tactics, to let me always know I'm being watched, and watched closely. The news that it had also scared my neighbour a little wasn't nice for me to know. Also not nice to know is occasionally we get up to things that adults get up to in our lounge, it's not nice to know there's some pervert outside. After thirty years it was time to put a stop to this invasion of privacy. I can cope with my phone calls being monitored and all that kind of stuff. But sitting in my garden watching my wife, for me that's over the top. Time for me to do what I do best again. My hospital escape and the skills I used in that escapade needed to come out the drawer again, to put a stop to it all, once and for all.

I began that day to make my plans.

8.30 am one weekday, I arrived at John's shop in town, Castle Cameras, at the top of the main shopping street, Union Street, in Torquay. I picked the lock, even though I'm way out of practice, old skills soon come back. I didn't care people were walking past, every shop was opening up and staff arriving, with my body hiding the fact I had no key it didn't look too odd and nobody cares to take a second glance. As I entered the shop the alarm went off, it didn't matter, every day at this time shop alarms go off as staff are too slow to enter the code to turn the system off. This shop was likely to be one of several going off at that time of day and no one batted an eye. If you ever want to break into a shop, 8:30 am is a great time to do it. I did find the noise of the alarm a little intimidating, but I didn't let it worry me too much. I went through to the back of the shop where John had his film processing equipment. Here I sat and waited for John to arrive, I looked around, the shop was run down, people don't get film processed these days it's all digital, camera sales must be rock bottom, it was obvious to me that the shop was being supported and subsidised to keep it going, and probably just for my benefit, a cover for John's existence, what a ridiculous waste of taxpayers money. I was in a stern mood, this had to go well. I sat facing the front door, with the noise of the alarm I could not hear John arrive I needed to see the door. At 8:50 John appeared at the front door, looking mystified why his door was unlocked and the alarm sounding. He walked cautiously through the shop to the back room. Saw me sat looking at him, he was shaken but relieved it was me, he shouldn't be, I meant business today.

"Andy, hi, nice for you to let yourself in," he said as he entered the code to stop the noise. "For what do I owe this pleasure". Letting myself in wasn't normal, yes I came here often for a chat, we had the strange relationship of being best of friends, having dinners together with our partners, we had bar room banter in the yacht club, not as friends but rival crews, crews always stuck to their own boat, it was always competition time after the races in the bar.

"I'm here on business today John. I'm here to ask, no, tell you it's time for you to go back home to your house in Kent, it's enough don't you think" I stood up and placed my left hand on my buttock in a mock move that looked as though I'm about to take my Glock out again. John stepped back thinking he was about to join Jean's fate. I saw him glance at a draw in his workbench, I guessed he had a weapon or something in there, he was making the decision whether to make a move for it but realised he would be dead before he'd even touch the drawer handle, he'd seen me shoot before and knew I was good.

I needed to avoid a fight, I had to keep him under my control. "John, I'm telling you to go today, it's an offer you are not going to refuse. Look at yourself, your business is nothing, cameras have had their day, you smoke far too much crap, you are a disgrace to the Intelligence Service, I bet they sent you here because babysitting me is a nice easy job for you, you are not capable of anything more. How much money are they spending to keep you here, it's beyond ridiculous? So, to help you realise leaving town is your only option, I'm going to show you something. Here put this film through the processor" I said. In the middle of the room was the

Fujifilm processor, it developed the few films that customers brought in for printing these days. In the past we had fun looking at the bedroom pictures people had the nerve to send in, now it was all just film club stuff and very little of it.

John moved to take the film from me, I made the deliberate move around him to cut off his access to the work table drawer and whatever he has in it while keeping my left hand on my hip letting him know not to make a move on me. Once he had set up the film to feed into the machine, I'd had a quick glance at my watch, the timing was crucial to my plan. Shall we have a cup of tea I suggested, immediately I regretted it, now I was going to arm him with a pot of boiling water. I'd need to keep my eye on him for any sign he was thinking of making a move on me, but if I couldn't beat John in a draw or fight I would worry, he was six years older than me and years of smoking and drugs had taken its toll on him. John stuck the leader tape onto the end of the film protruding from the cartridge and loaded it into the processing machine, and started its C-41 journey through the machine, as it's called. I'd been here many times for a chat with John I could have done it myself but it was better he did it. Once done he made two mugs of tea, he didn't need to ask if I needed milk and sugar. He asked "So what's this about? What's the film for?" He looked and sounded very worried now, and quite sheepish, normally there was a bounce to his voice and always a smile. "You'll see soon enough, trust me John, you will be packing your bags today. I don't know what's happened to you John, we've been best friends and now I find you've been coming into my home, watching from my garden."

"You were meant to know that we are watching you, to stop you doing anything stupid"

"For thirty years John!"

"We never let up, you know that"

"Not me John, I'm no traitor. For God's sake, I've even helped you, remember, remember the time I taught you how to do my 'legally rob' the bank thing". I was referring to the time a retailer friend of his was in financial trouble, completely broke and the bailiffs were coming to his shop at the bottom of the town in Torquay. John and I helped the poor guy load all his shop's stock into a van overnight and hid it. In the morning the shop was empty for the bailiff. The guy was flat broke. In the days before debit and credit pin numbers and the bank tellers used a swipe machine that took a print of a debit card, I had discovered a way to walk into a bank, ask for a sum of money quite legally, take the cash and the money gets credited back to your account. That part is not quite so legal, but there is nothing the teller or the bank can do about it. It worked if you weren't greedy and asked for no more than £200. In those days that was a week's wages. I thought of the idea to use when, for instance, one wanted to stay in a hotel untraced. If one uses a debit or credit card the authorities instantly know where you are, or in those days a few days after the credit card chits are checked. Even if you take the cash they know where you are, but if it's refunded to your account there is no proof you have been anywhere. I used the method myself once. I taught John the method to get cash for his friend to get him to a new town where he could start a business with his van full of stock. It wasn't a technique I wanted to share openly, as although you did nothing illegal, it was morally wrong, well, perhaps, but I always enjoy seeing a fat bank getting stuffed, those establishments do nothing but cause misery to people, they create nothing. But I digress.

"I know Andy, but you know the business, they have ways to get you to do anything. They tell me to watch you, and I have to watch you."

"Not any longer John you have to go back to your home in Kent now," I said in quite a kind tone. The film finished passing through the machine. I took it and put it onto the print machine to convert the film to paper photographs, I knew how to do this, I had watched John so many times. At that moment Wayne, John's shop assistant entered the shop, late for work as ever. As he came into the back room I spoke to him "Wayne I'm sorry, John's a little upset, his business hasn't been doing too well, he has to close down. Go home, you will be paid any money due including any holiday pay owed. Go now, take a camera or something from the shop for yourself" Wayne looked at John who looked so pale now, John just nodded and Wayne left without saying a word. I checked my watch again, I finished my cup of tea, John spoke: "So come on, what have you got, are you going to kill me or what, get on with it?"

"So, take a look at these pictures," I said as I finished twelve prints "do you recognise this?" I showed him the first photo, "Yes, it's my house in Kent, how did you take that?" Clearly, as I have all my movements monitored he didn't know how or when I took the picture, "John, you know me and my skills, I can do stuff like this without being seen. Recognise this?" as I showed him another angle of his house again "Yes"

"It's your house yes, I'm telling you to go back there and don't come back"

"Why?" John still had no idea of my intentions.

"If you don't bad things are going to happen"

"Really, so what?"

"Who lives in your house?"

"My daughter Sarah, but she is away right now, on holiday in Florida"

"So, you recognise this picture" I showed him another picture this time of the interior, in the kitchen. "Yes, it's my kitchen"

"And what is on the kitchen table, here look at this picture it's a closer view"

"A clear plastic bag of marijuana? It's a big bag"

"Yes, it's about 10 ounces about £3,000 worth. It will last you a long time, it's yours, to tempt you home"

"Don't be silly that won't make me go" John laughed pretending he could resist a stash like that, he couldn't.

"So Sarah comes home in 3 days, yes?"

"Yes, how do you know that?"

"It doesn't matter how I know. So you have 3 days to pick it up or she finds it on the table, and just by coincidence, the police may be passing by just as she finds it. Get my drift?"

"I'll just call someone to go get it" John tried to laugh off my bribe. With perfect timing, the shop phone rang at that moment.

"That will be for you John, a little push to help you leave" With that, John answered the phone, it was his son Peter. Peter was the manager of the Castle Inn, Totnes, just opposite John's house but not for much longer.

"Dad, I need help, can you call someone for me, the police are raiding my pub, they have found quantities of cocaine. Enough to accuse me of being a supplier.".

John turned to me "You bastard" I shrugged my shoulders with indifference.

"Agree to go and the problem will go away," I said "Go get your prize in Kent"

"I can order you dead" John tried to scare me

"No, you won't, no one will want to, because I have this" I showed John the next photo.

"A map?"

"Yes, recognise it? It's Northern Ireland"

"And?"

"Dots in fields, dots in fields," I said as I pointed to dots penned onto the map. John immediately knew what it was. During the Northern Ireland troubles, John had controlled an Increment.

Usually spying is secret and silent, when something needs to go loud and noisy or assassinations are the order of the day that work goes to what's called an Increment or The Increment. It can be specialists such as the SAS or snipers. If ever I needed to Increment a job, my preference was to use soldiers that fail SAS selection for a good reason, there can be many reasons to fail the tough selection course they are subject to. My reasoning was as soon as they get RTU'd or Returned to Unit, they are disappointed and when I approached them on platform 1 at Hereford Station, the platform that takes them home, and tell them I have a way for them use the skills they have, they are very often keen to do the specialised dangerous work, to prove they can do the job they so much want to do.

Margaret Thatcher's hotly denied shoot to kill policy in Northern Island existed, a small group of specialist men worked from a portacabin inside the grounds of the Maze Prison. They would go out into the towns, pick up a man wanted for a crime that could not be proven in court, usually an IRA associate, take him into the countryside, where a friendly farmer had dug a trench. The poor man as he walked into the field would be shot in the back of his head and dumped into the mass grave. The farmer then filled in that part of the trench and dig another for the next victim. Highly secret and controversial, this practice had been vehemently denied. Only since Thatcher died have rumours re-emerged.

This map was proof that the policy did exist and showed the locations of the mass graves, I believe there are at least 30 men in one.

John was the controller of the policy, I knew it, and he never knew I knew, until now.

"This is my insurance that no one touches me. The map has been deposited with a solicitor. If anything happens to me or any of my family, the map goes public." I knew this map should never be made public, but I needed to protect myself. I have been in the business too long to know what can happen.

"Agree to go now and I make a phone call and Pete can go free too"

"Ok, Andy you win. I'll go" John was beaten. I took my mobile from my pocket and made the call

"Andy here, you are at the Castle Inn still? Good, let Pete go free, I have the information I need, he is not to be touched. Thank you." Ok, John, Pete is free and no repercussions.

"Cunt" was John's last words to me.

"Goodbye John"

2018 was also the year my father died, he was the only person in my family that knew and witnessed some of my adventures. He was the only family member to have entered Century House when I returned from Angola with so many injuries. With his passing went the only person reliable enough to confirm my story. At his funeral, neither of my brothers wanted to speak or say anything. For the first time, I fought against my instinct to remain at the back of the room, invisible and silent. I wrote my Dad's eulogy and spoke at the funeral. Others had spoken before telling the story of my Dad's life, I promised a eulogy that would be something new and surprising. So in front of 150 people, family and friends, I revealed his story, how he had kept my past secret from them all too. I stood at the front of them all and saw 150 unbelieving faces. I looked, as I spoke, mostly at Jurate, she had no idea what I was going to speak about, her face remained blank, giving me no clue whether I was doing the right thing. I started to shake again as I spoke to the gathered friends and family, as I used to after Angola, but the shaking left me when I finished speaking and has never returned.

The positive thing about my 'coming out' has been that in myself I am perfectly happy now. I have some kind of closure, people don't understand it. Yes, people think I'm a fantasist that I've made it all up. I'm not going to cry over that, because only I know the true story of Andrew Gilbrook.

An Ordinary Guy, An Unknown Spy.

38. End Note

The UNAVEM mission, later renamed UNAVEM I was established by Security Council resolution 626 (1988) of 20 December 1988 at the request of the Governments of Angola and Cuba. Its task was to verify the redeployment of Cuban troops northwards and their phased and total withdrawal from the territory of Angola, in accordance with the timetable agreed between the two Governments. The withdrawal was completed by 25 May 1991 – more than one month before the scheduled date.

Two other UNAVEM missions were established following the first, UNAVEM II established May 1991 until February 1995. The mission was "*to verify the arrangements agreed by the Angolan parties for the monitoring of the ceasefire and the monitoring of the Angolan police during the ceasefire period*". In March 1992 the mandate was altered to include electoral monitoring duties. UNAVEM II suffered a total of 5 fatalities, 3 military and 2 civilians.

UNAVEM III February 1995 - June 1997 The mandate was to ensure ceasefire between the Angolan Army and the UNITA rebels and then arrange for a safe "quartering" of these UNITA rebels once they laid down their arms.

Peace has eluded Angola for four decades. The conflict has seamlessly transformed itself from an independence struggle against Portuguese colonisers to a well-funded war drawing in both superpowers, and finally, into an even deadlier and more devastating contest for personal power and resources. For Angolans, the tragedy has been overwhelming: more than five hundred thousand have been killed and more than half of the country's population of 10 million has been displaced by war.

The search for peace and reconciliation in Angola stretched for more than 10 years. The thawing of the Cold War in the late 1980s, combined with the military stalemate between UNITA and the MPLA, as well as the war-weariness among Angolan people, created seemingly favourable conditions for a political settlement. The Bicesse Peace Accords, mediated by Portugal with the assistance of the US and Russia, were signed on May 31 1991. The accords were hailed from Washington to Moscow as a model for post-Cold War peace-making. However, within a year the carefully constructed 63-page peace accord had become a lesson on what to avoid in a new era of peace-making - the country had entered a new and bloodier phase of the conflict.

The Lusaka Accords were signed in November 1994. The signing came after 12 months of negotiations and was an attempt to correct what were assumed to be the fatal flaws of the Bicesse Accords. The Lusaka agreement mandated a flexible demobilisation time frame, provided provisions for power-sharing, and gave the UN sufficient muscle and money to implement the accords. In December 1998, after a tenuous four-year ceasefire, the accords collapsed and the country plunged back into full-scale war.

Against a background of constant conflict and failed peace attempts the Angolan conflict boasts few successes and provides myriad examples of pitfalls in the negotiation process.

Comandante Anselmo Gil officially died as a consequence of his position in a dangerous mission, there were others killed too on that mission. It was an easy matter for MI6 to cover up the real story of who he was. As are murders in London. He was awarded a UNAVEM Angola medal posthumously, even though to qualify he should have been in Angola for 6 months. Somehow the medal found its way to me. Telling me, that MI6 is still involved in the UN in some dark and covert way.

Are there any other MI6 stories I can tell? Quite likely.

Back cover picture: The UNAVEM Medal presented to Anselmo Gil posthumously. Whoever was inside the UN, and quite possibly an agent under Roger's control, received this medal for Anselmo and passed it through various people to reach me, I have possession of this medal.

Printed in Great Britain
by Amazon